EASTERN'S ARMAGEDDON

Recent Titles in
Contributions in Labor Studies

EASTERN'S ARMAGEDDON

Labor Conflict and the Destruction of Eastern Airlines

Martha Dunagin Saunders

Contributions in Labor Studies, Number 42

GREENWOOD PRESS
Westport, Connecticut • London

HE
9803
E2
528
1992

Library of Congress Cataloging-in-Publication Data

Saunders, Martha Dunagin.
    Eastern's armageddon : labor conflict and the destruction of
Eastern Airlines / Martha Dunagin Saunders.
        p.   cm.—(Contributions in labor studies, ISSN 0886-8239 ;
no. 42)
    Includes bibliographical references and index.
    ISBN 0-313-28454-7 (alk. paper)
    1. Eastern Air Lines, inc.—Reorganization. 2. Eastern Air Lines,
inc.—Personnel management. 3. Lorenzo, Frank. 4. Strikes and
lockouts—Airlines—United States. I. Title. II. Series.
HE9803.E2S28 1992
387.7'06'573—dc20   92-9581

British Library Cataloguing in Publication Data is available.

Library of Congress Catalog Card Number: 92-9581
ISBN: 0-313-28454-7
ISSN: 0886-8239

First published in 1992

Greenwood Press, 88 Post Road West, Westport, CT 06881
An imprint of Greenwood Publishing Group, Inc.

Printed in the United States of America

The paper used in this book complies with the
Permanent Paper Standard issued by the National
Information Standards Organization (Z39.48-1984).

10 9 8 7 6 5 4 3 2 1

TO EASTERN AIRLINES

1928–1991

CONTENTS

PREFACE

This book examines the escalation of an organizational conflict to one of the most talked about industrial crises of our time. Through an analysis of the messages exchanged by some of its key participants—the pilots and management representatives of Eastern Airlines—this study attempts to explain how and why some 4,000 men and women walked away from high-paying glamour jobs, and toppled an institution. This book is *not* an evaluation of the economic climate or financial events that put Eastern into a critical bind. Instead, it is an analysis of the human cost of an organizational tragedy which, according to many observers, could have been avoided.

The present analysis is useful for two reasons:

1. The problem of organizational unrest in the United States is growing. Since World War II, there have been

10,807 work stoppages.[1] In June 1989, 21 work stoppages were in effect involving 148,500 workers. Experts say changes in the workplace resulting from mergers, takeovers, and acquisitions over the next ten years will be characterized by increasing volatility.[2] Conflict, although inevitable within and between organizations, produces dysfunctional consequences. "It can reduce productivity, decrease morale, cause dissatisfaction, and increase tension and stress in the organization."[3] Although strikes are the principal overt manifestations of conflict, their actual costs are overshadowed by the ill effects produced by persistent interpersonal and intergroup tensions preceding them.[4] Increasingly, proactive methods for dealing with crises are being called for by organizational specialists.

2. Although the concept of conflict as a research issue has become important in organizational studies in recent years, little effort has been made to establish a broad gauge for measuring communication efforts during intraorganizational conflict.

While it is widely assumed that a connection exists between persuasive messages and organizational change, research has not fully identified what the form or extent of that connection is. Theories of social change tell us that communications among individuals seeking change from established systems follow rather precise recipes; I believe these "recipes" are followed as well by individuals within organizations. Therefore, the central question of this study is whether the demise of Eastern Airlines was preceded by detectable patterns of communication between pilot groups and management in which the pilots' attempts to redress grievances and seek change were dealt with in an increasingly cooperative or noncooperative manner. This book goes beyond superficial observations of the phenomenon of organizational crisis and attempts to discover a methodological framework for observing the behaviors of the participants in organizational conflict as they engage in strategies of change.

This book will be of interest to the *organizational specialist* whose responsibility extends to creating effective communication strategies for internal as well as external publics; to the *social scientist* interested in patterns of communication during conflict; and to *students of collective action*, or anyone interested in the process of change.

Eastern Airlines has provided the setting for my research since 1986. Specifically, I have studied events involving the pilots of Eastern which led to a mass walkout in 1989 and the ultimate demise of the company. My interest in those issues is two-fold. First, a strike by a professional group is compelling because, simply put, professional groups don't often go on strike, and such a situation offers a rare opportunity for observation. Second, as a communicator I hold an abiding interest in the messages generated by participants in organizational disputes. That interest, combined with fifteen years of association with Eastern, encouraged the development of this study.

I would like to thank Kristy Gilmore, my research

assistant, who contributed countless hours coding data, and who served as sounding board and reality check throughout the process; Bob Saunders, Frank Grassi, and Belinda Maynard who provided valuable documentation, and whose observations enhanced the external validity of this study; and Joe Bailey who took over as "mother of the year" while I was working on this manuscript. I owe you, Joe.

Financial support for this project was provided in part by the University of West Florida's Committee on Research and Creative Activities.

NOTES

1. Department of Labor, Bureau of Labor Statistics, *Monthly Labor Review* (Washington, D.C.): Department of Labor, Bureau of Labor Statistics, 1989), 39.

2. Carol Kinsey Goman, *Strategies to Excel in Changing Times* (Berkeley, Calif.: Kinsey Consulting Services, 1986).

3. Judith R. Gordon, *A Diagnostic Approach to Organizational Behavior* (Boston, Mass.: Allyn & Bacon, 1987), 475.

4. Arthur Kornhauser, Robert Dubin, and Arthur M. Ross (eds), *Industrial Conflict* (New York: McGraw-Hill, 1954), 15.

INTRODUCTION

In February 1986, the fifty-eight year existence of Eastern Airlines as an independent company came to an end. Following years of turmoil, Eastern was sold to Texas Air Corporation (TAC), a holding company that owned Continental Airlines, People Express, and New York Air. A period of severe employee unrest followed. In March 1989, a strike against the airline was called by the International Association of Machinists and was supported by both the Transport Workers Union, representing the flight attendants, and the Air Line Pilots Association. A week later, Eastern filed for bankruptcy and its management fought to retain control over Eastern in the face of furious resistance from labor and rapidly diminishing confidence among its investors.

On April 18, 1990, bankruptcy court judge Burton Lifland ruled that Frank Lorenzo, the brash corporate raider who had acquired Eastern for his Texas Air empire, was unfit to run the company and appointed a trustee for the airline. A last ditch effort for order failed, and on January 18, 1991, the company folded its wings for good.

Industry analysts agree that the solidarity of the unions, especially the support of the pilots, contributed greatly to the defeat of Frank Lorenzo. Air Line Pilots' Association attorney Bruce Simon was quoted as saying: "Lorenzo is not in a position to set wage patterns in the industry anymore . . . . There has been a mood in this country over the past decade that you can beat up on unions and get away with it. The message here is that maybe you still can, but not in the airline industry. That is a major victory."[1] The "victory" referred to by Simon seems somehow less grand when one considers that most of the 42,000 people employed by Eastern when Lorenzo acquired it were put out of work. The industry may have been rid of a monster when Frank Lorenzo lost power, but the price paid by the people of Eastern was dear.

The pilots' efforts during the conflict were surprising to some observors. *The New Republic* reported:

> Traditionally, commercial airline pilots do not strike. They consider themselves professionals. Many have military backgrounds, and observe a military ethic and even etiquette. Yet . . . as management-labor relations at Eastern came to a crisis, it was the pilots who took a full-page advertisement

in *USA Today* listing the reasons why Texas Air is not "fit, willing, and able" to operate Eastern.[2]

Indeed, Eastern's management underestimated the extent of the pilots' discontent. "Management never thought the pilots would walk," said Belinda Maynard, a former member of Eastern's corporate communications staff. "In fact, they laughed at the suggestion that those guys would jeopardize their big paychecks. Boy, were they ever wrong!"

To many of the pilots, the conditions under which they were having to work at Lorenzo's Eastern were intolerable. They viewed the new owners as callous brutes, intent on despoiling the airline. Emotions ran deep. One pilot reflected the apparent views of many when, in response to a 1987 survey (two years before the strike), he responded gallantly:

[I am] greatly affected by current problems. I make less money than other pilots, but most of all I feel that the public thinks I work for a second class outfit. *This is not true!* Eastern Airlines has always been a great company to work for and I hate for people not to realize this. I will be honest with you, I consider Eastern as my family and I will defend this company as fiercely as a brother will fight for his sister. I think what hurts is when management comes and goes and takes their big slice of financial reward and we do not serve the public any better, really, and the workers are getting discouraged."[3]

The events leading to the pilot walkout at Eastern in 1989 were tumultuous, and the decision to support the IAM's strike was difficult, but as one former Eastern co-pilot commented, "We did what we thought we had to do. The eyes of an industry were on us. We were being cannibalized by our own parent [Texas Air]. Too many people were suffering. It wasn't about money or days off or anything like that. For us, walking out in support of the machinists was a point of honor!"

THE PRESENT STUDY

The goal of this study is to illuminate the communication behaviors and interactions between a labor group—in this case, the pilots of Eastern Airlines—and a company's management during a developing crisis; to thereby shed some light on the manner in which communication functions during intraorganizational conflict; and to establish a theoretical framework for the observation of similar events.

Chapter 1 presents a brief history of Eastern Airlines and includes a chronology of important events leading to the demise of the airline.

Chapter 2 discusses how communication strategies were used during the period immediately following the acquisition by Lorenzo's Texas Air Corporation. In addition, Chapter 2 provides some observations on the ultimate failure of the pilots' resistance efforts.

Chapter 3 points out the solidification activities of the

pilots during the period of relative peace following investor approval of the sale to TAC.

Chapter 4 follows the pilots' final push to unseat Lorenzo, up to the time of the walkout in 1989, and includes a look at the dynamics of an organizational rebellion.

Chapter 5 reveals the furious communication activity that occurred as the pilots joined with other unions and fought to wrest control of the bankrupt airline in order to prevent any further loss of assets.

Chapter 6 discusses the consequences faced by the pilots after they called off their strike only to find their jobs were no longer available.

Chapter 7 provides observations on organizational crisis and discusses the theoretical aspects of this study.

To examine the process of conflict escalation surrounding Eastern's pilot walkout, information on the controversy was collected by analyzing (1) the content of news stories involving the pilots or issues of interest to the pilots from January 1986 to January 1991; (2) articles gathered from *The Falcon*, Eastern's internal newsletter; (3) *Eastern Pilot's Checklist*, a newsletter developed by the Eastern pilots' Master Executive Council in 1987; and (4) virtually every letter, memorandum, and video directed to the pilots by both company and union sources.

This examination of the patterns of conflict between Eastern's pilots and management relies heavily on a theory of communication and social change known as the Bowers and Ochs theory of agitation and control. This theory has been used frequently as a tool for observing social conflict of the kind which occurred during the civil rights movement in the sixties, or the anti-Vietnam War activities of the seventies. Its usefulness as a gauge for measuring intergroup communication during organizational conflict emerged during the course of this study and will be demonstrated in subsequent chapters of this book.

In their book, *The Rhetoric of Agitation and Control*, John Waite Bowers and Donovan J. Ochs identify three primary aspects of conflict: *rhetoric*, *agitation*, and *control*, Their definitions for these terms were accepted for this study.

Rhetoric, as defined by Bowers and Ochs, extends beyond traditional definitions to include nonverbal communication (e.g., carrying signs, shaking fists). Specifically, the authors refer to rhetoric as *"the rationale of instrumental, symbolic behavior."*[4] The unit of analysis for the content analytic portion of this study, *the rhetorical event*, is based on this definition.

"Agitation exists," according to the authors, "when (1) people outside the normal decision-making establishment, (2) advocate significant social change, and (3) encounter a degree of resistance within the establishment such as to require more than the normal discursive means of persuasion."[5]   The communication behaviors of the pilots at Eastern Airlines, as they attempted to effect changes within the company, fall within this definition.

Control refers to the "response of the decision-making establishment to agitation."[6]   For the purpose of this study, all communication by Eastern's management regarding the company's pilots or issues of concern to the pilots, were considered examples of control behavior. Specific strategies of agitation and control behavior identified by the authors in their conflict model were used as categories for this analysis.

Bowers and Ochs identified specific strategies that agitative groups often adopt in their attempts to bring about change, as well as strategies employed by establishments to resist that change. These categorizations were especially useful in framing this research.

From the perspective of the theory, the pilots and management of Eastern were faced with a number of behavioral options as they addressed the conflict resulting from the acquisition. According to Bowers and Ochs, agitation (the pilots') activity could fall into one of nine categories, or strategies, of communication behavior: "petition of the establishment; promulgation; solidification; polarization; nonviolent resistance; escalation/confrontation; guerrilla and Gandhi; guerrilla; and revolution." The authors believed these strategies are generally cumulative and progress. That is to say, the strategies occur in the order they appear on the list (see Table 1).[7]

The first strategy available to an agitating group is *petition of the establishment*. This strategy represents the ordinary method of representing a case to the establishment. By definition, petitioning of the establishment does not constitute agitation. However, unless this strategy is used early in the agitative process, the

Table 1

Strategies and Sample Tactics Characteristic of Agitative Behavior

PETITION
    Phone calls
    Meetings with management

PROMULGATION
    Informational picketing
    Press releases/press conferences

SOLIDIFICATION
    Songs
    Slogans

POLARIZATION
    Flag issues (safety, union busting)
    Flag individuals (Frank Lorenzo)

NONVIOLENT RESISTANCE
    Prolonging departures
    Refusal to fly

ESCALATION/CONFRONTATION
    Threatened disruption, threatening to strike,
    Non-negotiable demands

GANDHI/GUERRILLA

GUERRILLA

REVOLUTION

movement is not likely to get off the ground. The establishment can point to the agitative group that has *not* gone through the petitioning process and lable them as "irresponsible firebrands who disdain normal decision-making processes in favor of disturbance and disruption."[8]

The strategy of petition is an important part of the agitative process, although not considered agitation, *per se*.

Here is rhetoric in its traditional *discursive* form, i.e., formal discourse—communication of thought and attitudes through either the written or spoken form. The "normal discursive means of persuasion" included as occurring within this strategy consists of lobbying efforts, letters to the establishment, meetings with the establishment, and petitions. Unless the agitator can show he or she has gone through the normal channels of persuasion, "he is unlikely to win support for or by the more drastic strategies."[9]

When the petitioning strategy is met by avoidance or suppression, the agitator will likely proceed to the next strategy—that of *promulgation*. It is this strategy in which the agitator seeks to win social support for his or her position. Utilizing such tactics as informational picketing, erection of posters, and distribution of handbills and leaflets, the agitator attempts to inform as many possible sympathizers as he or she can.[10]

Note that in this stage there is an admixture of *verbal* and *nonverbal* symbolism. The agitator's purpose for this strategy is to win public awareness, acceptance, and

support. This strategy includes also the tactic of *exploi-*
tation of the mass media—a tactic shared by all suc-
ceeding strategies.

This is an important tactic, because the promulgation
tactics defined in the preceding paragraph reach relatively
few people. The mass media reach a broader public,
thereby appealing to the agitator seeking to amass the
greatest support. This promulgation tactic is problematic
because, in the minds of editors, ideologies generally
make dull reading. Therefore, in order to create the kind
of conflict the media finds newsworthy, agitators often
have to resort to sensational tactics. In an effort to obtain
media attention, agitators often look for people within the
establishment who will endorse some of the agitators'
ideology. In addition, agitators often plan events for the
precise purpose of attracting media attention.[11]

The strategy of *solidification* takes place within the
agitating group and includes tactics designed to produce
or reinforce cohesiveness among the members. Tactics
such as songs, slogans, rallies, symbols, in-group
publications, buttons, and bumper stickers are used at
this stage to solidify members of an agitating group.
Examples of nonverbal solidification symbols from recent
movements include the raised fist of Black Power, two
fingers raised in the peace sign, and the thunderbird of
the National Farm Workers.[12]

The fourth strategy available to agitating groups is
polarization. The basis of this strategy is the assumption
that anyone who isn't for us must be for the establishment. The two main tactics used within this strategy are

the use of flag issues and flag individuals for exploitive purposes. These include issues and individuals who, for one reason or another, are especially susceptible to the charges made against the establishment by the agitator's ideology. For example, during the Vietnam war, flag individuals included President Lyndon Johnson, Secretary of State Dean Rusk, and Secretary of Defense Robert McNamara because the public perceived them as having most to do with forming and perpetuating American foreign policy. The primary flag issue among antiwar demonstrators was the killing with napalm of Vietnamese civilians, including women and children.[13]

Another polarizing tactic is "the *invention of derogatory jargon* for establishment groups."[14] Labor union members call replacement personnel "scabs." Exploiting factories are called "sweat shops," and management sympathizers and police are called "goons, ginks and company finks."[15] This tactic is reflective, of course, of the classic tactic of demogogic rhetoric, name-calling. The name for the tactic—expressed a bit more formally—is the *ad personam* argument—i.e., argument "at the person." It appears that in an agonistic setting—with both sides bent on "success"—the "argument" will inexorably deteriorate into *ad personam*. Ironically, it can be seen in the factional fights of the Christian churches.

The next strategy available to the agitation is *nonviolent resistance*. At this point, the agitator deliberately breaks laws or rules he or she considers to be unjust. This strategy was used effectively by Mahatma Gandhi and Martin Luther King, Jr.   Rent strikes, hunger strikes, sit-ins, and boycotts are methods of nonviolent resistance. This strategy can only be effective if agitation has adequate membership. There must be sufficient agitators so that the strike or sit-in will be annoying enough to have an effect.[16]

The strategy of *escalation/confrontation* follows next, in which the agitation attempts to make the establishment so apprehensive it overprepares for agitation, causes confusion, and is made to look foolish.[17] This strategy is relatively new to agitative rhetoric, according to Bowers and Ochs, and must be carefully planned and executed. Successful use of rumor and an underground press is important in the escalation effort. Tactics used include the following:

1. *Contrast*, so that the establishment will think a lot of agitators are going to appear, whether or not that will really happen
2. *Threatened disruption*
3. *Nonverbal offensive*—dressing strangely, and expressing sentiments (verbally or nonverbally) that are offensive to the establishment
4. *Verbal obscene deprecation*
5. The presentation of *non-negotiable demands*
6. *Nonverbal obscenity*, for example, spitting at security guards
7. *Token violence*[18]

The last three agitation strategies are *Gandhi and*

guerrilla, guerrilla, and *revolution.* The strategy of
Gandhi and guerrilla confronts the establishment with a
large group of agitators committed to the strategy of
nonviolent resistance and another group committed to
physical destruction of the establishment. The strategy assumes that the activities of each group will contribute to
the achievement of common goals. The strategy of
guerrilla includes physical underground attacks on the
establishment. These acts may serve as demonstrative
symbols to others. The strategy of *revolution* is not agitative in the classic sense. It is war.[19]

Bowers and Ochs begin an explanation of control
(management) strategies available to an organization by
pointing out principles governing the stance taken by an
establishment. That is, establishment leaders must
assume that any given instance of agitation will result in
the worst possible outcome. Establishment leaders must
be prepared to turn back any attack on the establishment.[20]

The authors maintain that when an establishment is
confronted with a proposal for change, it can adopt one
of four rhetorical strategies: *avoidance, suppression,
adjustment,* or *capitulation* (see Table 2).[21]

The strategy of *avoidance* includes a number of
tactics. *Counterpersuasion,* for example, involves talks
with the agitation leadership in an attempt to convince
them they are wrong.[22] This method is successful even
when it is unsuccessful in that it allows the establishment
to gain time and avoid any significant revision of establishment structure.

Table 2

Strategies and Sample Tactics Characteristic of Control Behavior

ADJUSTMENT
Changing name of agency
Sacrificing personnel
Accepting some of the means of agitation
Incorporating some of the personnel of agitation
Incorporating parts of the dissident ideology (agree to some terms)

AVOIDANCE
Counterpersuasion (taking under advisement, looking into, discussions, rebuttals)
Evasion (buckpassing, run around, refusal to comment, refusal to meet)
Postponement
Seeking public support, accusations, laying blame
Legal actions

SUPPRESSION
Harassment (suspensions, threatening bankruptcy or layoffs)
Preparing for strike, (training replacement pilots)
Firings

CAPITULATION

Counterpersuasion is the most common and often successful maneuver available to an establisment. The counterpersuasion tactic allows the establishment to shift into adjustment more gracefully than any of the other control tactics.[23]

Large organizations can use the tactic of *evasion*, often called "buckpassing," or "runaround." These organizations successfully avoid consideration of proposed change by simply routing agitation leaders through a maze of receptionists, secretaries, and assistants. Evasion is a risky tactic for an establishment. A powerful agitative movement can appeal to a higher, more powerful establishment.[24]

Smaller organizations, unable to use the tactic of evasion, often choose *postponement* as a method for deferring decisionmaking. This is done through taking requests to a board of directors of a committee, or under advisement, or forming *ad hoc* committees to review the situation.

Secrecy with a rationale is another tactic of avoidance. This occurs when an establishment declines to respond to a request for change by appealing to a higher principle. The authors use, as an example, American car manufacturers' refusal to reveal the actual manufacturing cost of an automobile because competitors could undercut their prices. National security has often been offered as a rationale for refusal to respond to questions involving military decisions.

Any establishment can also choose *denial of means* as a method of avoidance. In order to spread their ideas, agitative group members must have the physical means to do so. For example, paper, ink, and meeting halls are necessary for disseminating agitative ideas.[25] As an 2avoidance tactic, denial of means can be effective.

The next strategy available to an establishment in responding to external challenge is *suppression*. This strategy is not usually used unless avoidance tactics have failed. Tactics within this strategy are designed primarily to weaken or remove the movement's leaders.[26]

An early tactic of suppression is often *harassment* of the agitation's leaders. Harassment is designed to reduce the solidarity of the agitating group's membership. Another includes overt *denial of the agitator's demands*. Both tactics are risky, in that they may inflame agitators to push more vigorously than before. Two other suppressive tactics available to establishments are *banishment* and *purgation*.[27] This tactic can include excommunication, expulsion, academic suspension, exile, and incarceration.

Banishment may be the most effective suppressive tactic available to an establishment because without leadership most agitative movements simply fade away.[28] Purgation, the killing of leaders and members of the agitative movement, was used during the Boxer Rebellion of 1900, during the Hungarian Freedom Fighters demonstration in 1956, and more recently during the Chinese student demonstrations in Beijing in 1989.

A third strategy available to the establishment is *adjustment*, during which institutions alter their structures to meet some of the demands of the agitation. It is important that the adjustment not be perceived as a concession or partial surrender by establishment supporters.[29] An establishment can adjust by *sacrificing personnel*, a tactic often used when agitation is addressed to a flag person. Lyndon Johnson may have used this tactic when he stepped down from the presidency following antiwar demonstrations in 1967-68.[30] Another tactic of adjustment is *changing the name of the regulatory agency* in order to seemingly yield to agitation demands. For example, after students of one college demonstrated against Dow Chemical and Marine recruiters, the campus Business and Industrial Placement Office was renamed the Office of Career Counseling.[31]

Other adjustment tactics available to establishments include *incorporation of some of the personnel of the agitative movement*, and *incorporation of parts of the dissident ideology*. These tactics may be substantial or token.[32]

The last strategy available to an institution, *capitulation*, occurs as an establishment's last resort and does not occur voluntarily. Capitulation, according to Bowers and Ochs, means total defeat.[33]

In order to predict outcomes during specific instances of agitation and control, Bowers and Ochs first isolated three variables for agitation and control. The authors then manipulated those variables in an effort to explain what apparently takes place in real agitative situations.[34]

According to the model, the variables critical to agitation are (1) actual membership, (2) potential membership, and (3) rhetorical sophistication. Actual membership in-

cludes the number of members considered active within
an agitative group. The authors argue that this number
always starts out small and that large actual membership
probably does not exist in an agitative movement.
Potential membership depends on the strength of the
agitative group's ideology and the number of people in
the society who may be receptive to that ideology.
Rhetorical sophistication is the extent to which agitative
leaders know and use basic principles of rhetoric.[35]

Variables critical to control are (1) power, (2) strength
of ideology, and (3) rhetorical sophistication. Power is
described as either referent or expert. Referent power is
power over a person when that person relates to the
individual or group in power. Expert power is the kind
of power that attracts influences because of a particular
skill or knowledge in some area which interests the in-
fluencee. By strength of ideology, the authors mean that
the establishment's ideology is logically consistent and
empirically valid. If this occurs, the establishment
remains strong. Logical consistency means that everyone
in the system shares the same set of values. The authors
recognize a vertical deviance type of agitation which
occurs in situations when the agitators have no quarrel
with the general value system of the establishment.[36]

In the Eastern Airlines scenario, actual membership,
or the number of active members in the agitative group,
was small initially. Potential membership can be considered high, in the case of the pilots, because of the
possibility of the pilots' union combining efforts with the
other major unions at Eastern. The rhetorical sophistica-

tion of the pilots became evident in their ability to attract and maintain media attention, as well as to launch their own publications and telecommunications network.

The Eastern establishment possessed a high level of referent and expert power, logical consistency in the form of unity, and coherence of beliefs within a value system, as well as rhetorical sophistication through a complex network of corporate communications.

On the basis of these variables, Bowers and Ochs developed a set of generalizations in an effort to predict the outcomes of agitative situations. One of these generalizations, which suited this analysis, occurs when the three variables are balanced between agitation and control When this happens, the establishment will almost always successfully avoid or suppress the agitation.[37]

This happens because the establishment holds the advantage in *legitimate power*.[38] Legitimate power, somewhat complex in definition, occurs when an individual or group perceives another as having a sort of social contract or charter over them. Through this position, the establishment can assert influence. Legitimate power is held by the establishment in every organization and is, in fact, a defining characteristic of the establishment.[39]

NOTES

1. Aaron Bernstein, *Grounded: Frank Lorenzo and the Destruction of Eastern Airlines* (New York: Simon and Schuster, 1990), 230.

2. Henry Fairlie, "Air Sickness," *The New Republic*, June 5, 1989, 21.

3. Martha Saunders, "Eastern's Employee Communication Crisis," *Public Relations Review* 14 (Summer 1988): 37-38.

4. John Waite Bowers and Donovan Ochs, *The Rhetoric of Agitation and Control* (Reading, Mass.: Addison-Wesley, 1971), 2.

5. Bowers and Ochs, 4.

6. Bowers and Ochs, 4.

7. Bowers and Ochs, 4.

8. Bowers and Ochs, 4.

9. Bowers and Ochs, 5.

10. Bowers and Ochs, 17.

11. Bowers and Ochs, 19-20.

12. Bowers and Ochs, 20.

13. Bowers and Ochs, 27.

14. Bowers and Ochs, 28.

15. Bowers and Ochs, 28.

16. Bowers and Ochs, 28-33.

17. Bowers and Ochs, 35.

18. Bowers and Ochs, 35.

19. Bowers and Ochs, 36-37.

20. Bowers and Ochs, 40.

21. Bowers and Ochs, 40.

22. Bowers and Ochs, 40.

23. Bowers and Ochs, 41.

24. Bowers and Ochs, 42.

25. Bowers and Ochs, 45.

26. Bowers and Ochs, 47.

27. Bowers and Ochs, 51.

28. Bowers and Ochs, 51.

29. Bowers and Ochs, 52.

30. Bowers and Ochs, 53.

31. Bowers and Ochs, 52.

32. Bowers and Ochs, 66.

33. Bowers and Ochs, 55.

34. Bowers and Ochs, 136.

35. Bowers and Ochs, 137.

36. Bowers and Ochs, 7-137 passim.

37. Bowers and Ochs, 7.

38. Bowers and Ochs, 141.

39. Bowers and Ochs, 13.

1

HISTORY AND CHRONOLOGY

> On January 1, 1935, a new general manager
> was named . . . whose name would forever
> be associated with the airline . . . . His
> name was Edward Vernon Rickenbacker.[1]

In his informal history of Eastern Airlines, *From the Captain to the Colonel*, Robert J. Serling writes:

> Eastern is a fascinating example of an airline whose
> past is both a proud legacy and a burden that time
> has failed to erase completely. More than any other
> airline in the world, Eastern is a Jekyll-and-Hyde
> company, a kind of schizophrenic corporation
> whose history and the chief characters who wrote
> that history are a collection of paradoxes, contrasts,
> and contradictions.[2]

Written during a time of relative stability within the organization, Serling's book provides many useful insights into the organizational framework and culture of the airline.

EARLY DAYS

Eastern Airlines (EAL) was founded by Harold Pitcairn, who shocked his wealthy family by announcing his intention of making a career and a business out of "the horrifyingly dangerous airplane."[3] "Civil aviation was virtually nonexistent in this country" when young Pitcairn soloed his first airplane in 1916. Planes were thought to be weapons of war by most people, although Tony Jannus had pioneered the notion of scheduled passenger service via airplane from St. Petersburg to Tampa, Florida, in 1914. (Jannus's St. Petersburg-Tampa Airboat Line lasted only four months).[4]

Pitcairn shared his dream with a young aeronautical engineer named Agnew Larson and together they developed a "trim, fast little plane" called the Fleet Aero. At that time, in the early 1920s, civil aviation consisted mainly of "barnstorming, stunt flying, and occasional charter trips."[5]

Everything changed in 1925 when the Contract Air Mail Act was passed. Sponsored by Pennsylvania Representative Clarence Kelly, the bill gave the job of flying the mail to private contractors. Thousands of bids began pouring in within weeks. Among the successful bidders was Pitcairn Aviation.[6]

By mid-1928, "Pitcairn was flying almost a third of the nation's total airmail mileage."[7] At that time, in a surprise move, Pitcairn sold the airline to Clement Keys, former editor for *The Wall Street Journal*. Keys moved the airline's headquarters to Brooklyn and changed its name to Eastern Air Transport officially on January 15, 1930.[8] In August of that year, Eastern began carrying passengers for the first time.[9]

Eastern followed a promotion gimmick of female cabin attendants started by United Aircraft. Although adamantly opposed by the pilots, twenty-two women were selected for the title of "hostess"—among them debutante Mildred Johnson and Mildred Aldrin, whose nephew Buzz found fame as an astronaut.

The qualifications were stiff—a lot stiffer than the training, which was nonexistent. Eastern accepted only unmarried women under twenty-eight; the height limit was five feet four inches and weight 123 pounds. An applicant had to be either a registered nurse or a college graduate—a prerequisite which few of them understood once they went to work on the menial tasks assigned to flight attendants in the 1930s.[10]

The Depression years brought adversities, but Eastern Air Transport remained relatively healthy until 1931 when Clement Keys went to Europe with visions of a global aviation empire. While he was gone, Keys's associates at his investment company diverted funds into the still-plunging stock market leaving Keys to face financial ruin. Keys saved the airline through negotiations with five banks—in exchange for his resignation.[11]

On January 1, 1935, a new general manager was named to (then called) Eastern Air Lines, whose name would forever be associated with the airline. Often called "a true visionary when it came to aviation," his name was Edward Vernon Rickenbacker.[12]

CAPTAIN EDDIE

Rickenbacker, an arch-conservative and former World War I flying ace, ruled the company with an iron fist for a quarter of a century and left to his successors "the most glittering record of any airline chief in aviation history: twenty-six consecutive years of profit, the last twenty-one without a penny of government subsidy."[13]

When Rickenbacker turned over the leadership of Eastern to Malcolm MacIntyre in 1959, the airline served 128 cities in 27 states emcompassing almost three-fourths of the American population. The 228 Falcons flew 1,400 separate trips a day, adding up to half a million miles every day. Its route system linked every major city from New England and the Great Lakes to Florida and the Gulf Coast, and from the Atlantic Seaboard and Puerto Rico to St. Louis and Texas.[14]

MacIntyre was a brilliant lawyer but had virtually no experience in the rough-and-tumble game of running a major airline. When he left office in 1963, Eastern was headed for financial oblivion, with net operating losses of $38 million. MacIntyre is also remembered for two bright spots in the company's history—the introduction of the Boeing 727 and the development of the Shuttle. The former became a workhorse for the industry, and the latter involved a brilliant customer relations strategy. The shuttle flights between New York, Washington, and Boston required no reservations and guaranteed a seat to anyone who showed up.[15]

The Shuttle immediately became a way of life for travelers moving between the heavily traveled Washington-New York-Boston corridor. The phrase "I'll catch the Shuttle" became commonplace. By 1978, the Shuttle was carrying two and a half million passengers a year—more passengers than the airline had flown in the entire decade of 1930-40.[16]

COLONEL BORMAN

In 1975 Eastern's fortunes were entrusted to the man who was called "the real inheritor of Captain Eddie's leadership mantle"—former astronaut Colonel Frank Borman.[17] As president and CEO, Borman brought charisma and a familiar military ethic back to Eastern. He negotiated considerable wage concessions from the employees in an attempt to save the company from disaster but failed to compensate for the exhorbitant cost of the new airplanes he had ordered or the costly effects of deregulation. Borman and Eastern's machinist unions chief, Charles Bryan, clashed furiously and frequently, although the pilots maintained some identification with Borman, the test pilot and astronaut.

For Borman, the economic troubles brought endless

conflicts with his employees. *Business Week* reporter
Aaron Bernstein noted, "Labor brawls struck Eastern
with the regularity of tropical storms in Florida."[18] The
debt he had incurred forced him to ask repeatedly for
concessions from his employees, and it hampered
company growth. "Borman would issue dire threats that
brought the unions to the very edge of a strike," Bernstein wrote. "Then he'd look at the balance sheet and
realize that if they walked off the job, the company
wouldn't be able to make the payments on its monumen-
tal loans. Facing bankruptcy, he would have no choice
but to back off."[19]

Many industry analysts blamed Eastern's troubles
partly on poor management and partly on the company's
uncooperative labor unions. A *New York Times Magazine* report explained:

> To be sure, the unions who see themselves as
> members of a family who have been victimized by
> successive cadres of bad managers, have made
> concessions as management lurched from one finan-
> cial crisis to another. But the concessions, accord-
> ing to financial analysts, have never gone deep
> enough . . . . [As a result] a lack of mutual faith
> has become deeply ingrained in the corporate
> culture.[20]

At the root of Eastern's troubles lay a poor route
structure and huge debt. It was as a result of these
seemingly incurable financial distresses combined with a

futile, eleventh hour grandstand play by Borman that Eastern succumbed to the takeover bid by Frank Lorenzo and his Texas Air empire.[21] The conflict over TAC's acquisition extended to several employee groups, notably the company's pilots, and proved to be the beginning of the end for Eastern.

CHRONOLOGY

A chronology of the events following Texas Air's acquisition of Eastern provides a useful reference for observing the strategies of agitation and control throughout this period.[22]

February 1986
● The pilots union reaches a tentative agreement with the firm following a threatened sale of the airline to TAC if its three unions did not agree to contract concessions.

● Company approves Texas Air acquisition bid, in spite of previous agreements.

June 1986
● Frank Borman resigns as chief executive officer and agrees to become vice-chairman and a director of Texas Air Corporation.

● Joseph Leonard becomes acting CEO.

September 1986

* Texas Air's acquisition of Eastern is approved by the Transportation Department.

October 1986

* Frank Lorenzo is named chairman. Phillip Bakes becomes president, CEO, and a director.

November 1986

* Eastern's employee unions file suit in U.S. district court to block Texas Air's pending acquisition of Eastern for $600 million in cash and notes. The suit alleges that Eastern's board of directors disregarded employees' interests and also claims that Texas Air swayed the board to accept the bid.

* Shareholders approve takeover at a special meeting which ended early because union members shouted down management.

December 1986

* Eastern files suit against the company's machinist union seeking to enjoin it from "unlawful proxy solicitation."

January 1987

* TAC folds its New York Air and People Express units into its Continental Airlines unit. This move consolidates TAC's operations into two almost equal-sized units, Continental and Eastern Airlines.

• TAC unveils a business plan that calls for sharp wage cuts.

February 1987
• Texas Air shifts six jumbo jets from Eastern Airlines to Continental Airlines revealing a willingness to move assets from its unionized subsidiary to its nonunion airlines.

March 1987
• A new Texas Air subsidiary, System One Holding, Inc., buys one of Eastern's biggest money makers, its computerized reservation system. Purchase price is $100 million (an estimated $100-$300 million below value). Eastern then is required to pay to use what it once owned.

April 1987
• FAA warns Eastern not to make its pilots fly more than the federal limit of thirty hours in a seven-day period. Federal administrators say that Eastern is currently not in accordance with FAA limits.

January 1988
• Pilots hire Touche Ross & Co., one of the country's largest accounting firms, to analyze Eastern's finances.

February 1988

● The AFL-CIO announces a broad campaign against TAC's chairman Frank Lorenzo, declaring that he has shown "unprecedented contempt" for his employees at the Eastern Airlines unit.

April 1988

● Eastern's unions sue the airline and Texas Air, claiming the companies campaigned to denude valuable assets and mislead stockholders—as part of a plan to drive organized labor out of Eastern.

● Eastern Airlines is temporarily grounded after FAA inspectors find safety violations.

May 1988

● Texas Air sues pilots' and machinists' unions charging them with leading an illegal conspiracy to destroy Eastern Airlines unit.

July 1988
● Eastern pilots propose work-rule concessions to management while continuing to press for pay increases.

August 1988

● Eastern's machinists' union gives firm's latest contract offer to its membership for a vote. Union leaders refuse to endorse offer.

October 1988
● Donald Trump agrees to buy Eastern Airlines shuttle service from TAC.

January 1989
● A mediated negotiating session between Eastern Airlines and its machinists' unions halts without resolution.

February 1989
● Machinists back call for strike in March.

March 1989
● Eastern offers pilots a new contract that company claims satisfies demands for job security to encourage pilots to cross machinists' picket lines.

● Strike begins March 4. Machinists are joined in sympathy by pilots and flight attendants.

● Eastern idles 7,000 nonunion workers and cancels nearly all flights.

● Courts refuse to order pilots back to work. Eastern furloughs another 2,500 employees.

● Eastern Airlines files for bankruptcy.

April 1989
● A group led by Peter V. Ueberroth and Eastern

announces the $464 million buyout proposal has col-
lapsed. Eastern says it intends to reorganize as a
smaller carrier.

May 1989
● A group led by William Howard, former chairman of Piedmont Aviation, discloses that it is
interested in making a buyout proposal for all of
Eastern. Chicago businessman Joseph Ritchie
already has expressed interest.

● Eastern graduates its first class of new pilots
hired since the start of the strike.

June 1989
● David Shapiro, bankruptcy examiner in the
Eastern case, dismisses the Howard group's offer.

● Eastern announces an austerity program for
nonunion employees.

● The Ritchie plan fails.

July 1989

● Pilots return to the bargaining table in order to
prevent Lorenzo from gaining permision to end the
pilots' contracts.

● Eastern submits a reorganization plan to the
bankruptcy court. Creditors approve.

August 1989
● Striking pilots vote to continue sympathy walk- *IV.*
out.

September 1989
● The striking pilots throw out their leader, Jack
Bavis, for proposing that they consider ending the   *IV.*
walkout.

● Lorenzo tells Texas Air shareholders that Eastern
will turn a profit in 1990.

November 1989
● Congress passes a bill to set up a bipartisan
commission to recommend a settlement at Eastern.
President Bush vetoes the bill.

● Pilots vote to end the union's sympathy strike but
are unable to return to jobs because they were taken *IV.*
by replacement pilots.

● Flight attendants agree to end their strike.   *IV.*

December 1989
● American Airlines announces it will buy Latin
American routes from Texas Air for $471 million.

January 1990
● Texas Air proposes a reorganization that calls for
paying creditors only fifty cents on the dollar.

April 1990
● Texas Air tells creditors it can only repay them at twenty-five cents on the dollar, with only five cents of it in cash. The rest would be in notes from Continental and Eastern.

● Creditors file a formal motion with Judge Lifland asking for a trustee.

● Judge Lifland appoints Martin Shugrue as trustee, stripping Lorenzo of power at Eastern.

January 1991
● Eastern Airlines ceases operations.

Beginning with the takeover bid by TAC, the following chapter, entitled "The Resistance," outlines the pilots' efforts to "save Eastern."

NOTES

1.   Robert J. Serling, *From the Captain to the Colonel: An Informal History of Eastern Airlines* (New York: Dial Press, 1980), 116.

2. Serling, 3.

3. Serling, 8.

4. Serling, 9.

5. Serling, 11.

6. Serling, 12.

7. Serling, 34.

8. Serling, 51.

9. Serling, 59.

10. Serling, 69.

11. Serling, 79.

12. Serling, 116.

13. Serling, 286.

14. Serling, 286.

15. Serling, 346.

16. Serling, 349.

17. Serling, 462.

18. Aaron Bernstein, *Grounded: Frank Lorenzo and the Destruction of Eastern Airlines* (New York: Simon and Schuster, 1990), 25.

19. Bernstein, 25.

20. William Stockton, "Tearing Apart Eastern Airlines," *New York Times Magazine*, November 6, 1988, 37-38.

21. Stockton, 38.

22. This chronology, collected from news accounts of the period, provides factual information by asking, "Who does what to whom?" Factual information such as this has not been shown to be distorted, according to M.H. Dantzger, "Validating Conflict Data," *American Sociology Review* 40 (October 1975): 570-584.

2

THE RESISTANCE

> He runs a sweatshop.
> —EAL pilot Ron Nelson, February 1986[1]

> Eastern will flourish under Lorenzo.
> —Larry Birger, *The Miami Herald*, June 1986[2]

In an essay by Don Huckabee, a "[too] early retired" Eastern captain, he argues:

One character in this melodrama who has received far too little public attention is former astronaut Frank Borman, the former Eastern chief executive officer (CEO), who laid the groundwork for the weekend midnight run when the other Frank [Lorenzo] made off with the spoils of Eastern.[3]

Huckabee reflected the apparent opinions of many pilots who accused Borman of selling out Eastern and its employees when he allowed the takeover by Frank Lorenzo:

Borman and Eastern's Board sold the airline on a weekend under dubious circumstances, disenfranchised the employees' 25 percent ownership, disallowed any other bidders, paid Lorenzo a nonrefundable $20 million inducement fee, and agreed to a process whereby Eastern paid 58 percent of its own acquisition costs.[4]

All this Borman did, according to Huckabee, "to sell to a man of questionable integrity where labor is involved."[5] Prior to the sale, Chairman Frank Borman had summoned the leaders of the Air Line Pilots Association (ALPA), Transport Workers Union (TWU), and International Association of Machinists (IAM) and had given them an ultimatum. He told them that if they were not able to come to any agreement by midnight Sunday, which was the date Frank Lorenzo's offer to buy would expire, he would sell the airline. In exchange for his promise not to sell, Borman demanded that the unions agree to 20 percent wage reductions for three years with no raises, reductions in vacations and benefits, and longer hours with more stringent work rules. The pilots settled, confident they could hold off the sale. The flight attendants followed suit and believed they had a deal. About an hour after midnight, IAM leader Charlie Bryan made an offer of a 15 percent pay cut **if** Borman would resign. The board refused and voted to sell the company.

Many of the pilots felt betrayed at the sale of their airline. Media reports reflected shock and horror across all levels of Eastern employees:

Eastern Airline pilot Ron Nelson turned on the Today Show Monday in his Coral Gables home and learned that his twenty-two years with the same employer were over.

Nelson arrived at work "in a state of shock."

"We've given, given, given and were ready to give again. But we got sold out," said Nelson after learning that his company may be purchased by Texas Air Corp., which runs what he called "a sweat shop."

"It takes people longer to sell a used car than they took to sell the country's third-largest airline," [Janet] McNeill [flight attendant] said.

Nelson blamed the sale on "Borman's ego."[6]

The eleventh hour effort to thwart the sale of the airline had failed. Many believed the sale was a "done deal" all along and that Borman had preyed upon their fears in order to gain last minute concessions. *The Miami Herald* reported the company may have deliberately prolonged its labor crisis by resurrecting contentious issues in order to make it appear that uncooperative unions had "forced" the sale, an accusation denied by company spokesmen.[7] Still, on June 1, 1986, Frank Borman resigned from Eastern to become vice chairman and a director of Houston-based Texas Air Corporation. His duties were not defined at the time, and he received a $900,000 cash severance payment from Eastern as well as consultant's fees of $150,000 per year until June 30, 1991. The severance and consulting agreement was disclosed in a proxy statement filed with the Securities and Exchange Commission, involving TAC's acquisition of Eastern.[8]

The day after Borman's resignation, Robert Shipner, chief pilot, was fired. A subsequent lawsuit stated that Shipner's relationship with Joseph Leonard (who succeeded Borman as president) had "deteriorated because of disagreements over Eastern's labor talks with ALPA."[9]

A second firing, that of Eastern's top labor and personnel executive Jack Johnson, further changed the profile of Eastern's management and sent a chill through the pilot ranks. Johnson had been well liked by the unions and, after years of battle with them, had earned their respect.[10] Both Shipner and Johnson were replaced by counterparts from sister carrier, Continental Airlines, also owned by Texas Air.

The U.S. Department of Transportation approved the

acquisition on October 2, prompting the unions to meet to review their options. The IAM pushed for an employee buyout, and the pilots joined in for a last-ditch effort. They asked Eastern's board of directors to reconsider the sale, sued to halt the sale, and, pushing harder, "informed a federal judge that they were prepared to offer $11.50 a share or $1.15 billion for the airline, if he would only break Texas Air's grip on 51 percent of Eastern's stock."[11] Federal judge Lawrence King denied any delay of the sale, and in November, "Eastern's tortuous life as an independent company came to a chaotic end . . . as shareholders attending its final annual meeting approved the carrier's takeover by Texas Air Corp."[12]

After failing to halt Texas Air's purchase of Eastern, the pilots, as part of a fledgling union coalition, asked for a meeting with company chairman Frank Lorenzo to discuss organizational plans. Lorenzo rejected the request.[13]

COMMUNICATION STRATEGIES OF PILOTS AND MANAGEMENT

Pilot Responses

The pilots responded to the takeover primarily through the agitative strategies of petitioning of the establishment, promulgation, and confrontation. Activities categorized as petitioning of the establishment, included normal means of persuasion.[14] In the case of the Eastern pilots, "normal" meant phone calls to management and union representatives; meetings between pilots (individual pilots, pilot groups, and group representatives) and Eastern's decision-making establishment; letters; and "talks" on specific issues between pilots and management. Petitioning activities at Eastern intensified as the pilots saw their worst nightmare coming true. The mere threat of association with TAC had kept them moving toward settlement. Frightened by the prospect of TAC chairman Frank Lorenzo as their boss, they plunged into negotiations.

Promulgating actions. or those activities designed to win social support for the pilots' position, included informational picketing; erection of posters; distribution of handbills, news clippings, and publications; mass protest meetings; press releases; press conferences; phone calls to the media; use of legitimizers; staged events and rallies; advertising, public relations, and publicity campaigns; personal interviews with the media; and public demands for meetings, debates, or talks. Utilizing this strategy, ALPA members picketed the Department of Transportation in Washington in protest of the absence of labor protective provisions. They paid for advertisements as a way of rebutting a series of ads taken out by the company.

The pilots made frequent use of the confrontational tactics of threatened disruption, which are common in labor disputes. Union leaders pushed hard from the beginning, grasping for every possibility to avoid the acquisition. Reports emerged that the investment banking firm of Lazard Freres & Co., which had been hired by ALPA, had asked Pan Am to consider making a rival bid shortly after Texas Air signed its deal with Eastern.

The agitative strategies of solidification and polarization were weak throughout the resistance. The pilots did ally themselves with the other unions and used the tactics of teleconferencing to keep in touch with membership; however, no real push to "band together and fight the tyrant" took hold at this time. This weakness was to be rectified, however, as pilots' perceptions of deprivation heightened over the coming months.

Dominant flag issues identified by the pilots in previous research included airplane safety, stability of the airline, and job security. The primary flag individual among the pilots was TAC chairman Frank Lorenzo, who was portrayed as a ruthless "union-buster."[15] Polarization efforts focused on Continental Airlines (also owned by TAC) as a dreadful example of what Lorenzo could do to an airline. Prior to the acquisition of Eastern, Lorenzo had successfully withstood a pilot strike at Continental and managed to have union contracts negated. Continental's nonunion pilots were known as "scabs" among Eastern's ALPA members. Lorenzo, according to the same group, was out to destroy labor unions and turn their company into a "sweatshop."[16]

Management's Responses

Eastern's management responded to the pilots' agitation most strongly through the avoidance tactics of counterpersuasion and evasion. The management practiced counterpersuasion by standing by one primary argument: "Our basic obligation is to run a profitable air-line."[17] Interaction between management and the pilots for the subsequent three years involved disagreements as to just how that obligation could and should be met.

Responding to a telegram sent to Lorenzo by union representatives, John Adams, Eastern's chief labor negotiator, wrote that "pre-conditions" set by the pilots, machinists, and flight attendants leaders "doom any efforts before they begin."[18]

Lorenzo's refusal to meet with pilots was an evasion tactic, as well as the frequent refusals to comment by company spokesmen. The firings of Shipner (chief pilot) and Johnson (Eastern's human resources vice president) could be interpreted as suppressive, if they were designed to deny pilots any friends in management.

The Falcon, Eastern's corporate communications newsletter, had generally been considered a credible, useful source of information by the employees until the time of the acquisition.[19] One month after the sale of the airline, *The Falcon* reported a teleconference between employees in seventeen cities and Frank Borman, chairman; Joe Leonard, president; and industry analyst John Pincavage. The article quoted serious concerns by some of the employees regarding the future of Eastern. As the year progressed, however, two-way communication of this nature ceased to be reflected in the pages of *The Falcon*.

CONCLUSIONS
By the end of 1986, all appeals had been denied.

Eastern Airlines became a part of Frank Lorenzo's Texas Air Corporation, and the pilots' efforts to thwart the takeover were lost. There were numerous reasons for the failure of the resistance, but this study suggests two salient aspects of this period that may have contributed to the defeat. First, the pilots were not strongly united in their response to the new management, neither had they ever been strongly united with the other unions. Although going through the motions of resistance activities, the average line pilot was in shock. It was difficult to comprehend that his way of life was in jeopardy. After all, hadn't the entire history of the company been fraught with turmoil? Surely this was just another in a long line of upheavals. Some of the pilots believed they should give new management a chance. After all, how much worse could things be?

Ironically, ALPA's national headquarters offered little advice to the rank and file throughout this period. ALPA national president Captain Henry A. Duffy said he shared "cautious optimism" with most Eastern pilots about Lorenzo's TAC becoming the new landlord of Eastern. "I informed him [Lorenzo] that we also wanted to restore Eastern to financial security and to continue the great heritage of this corporation, but that he would find us to be cautious observers, who would judge his deeds rather than his words."[20]

Air Line Pilot, the magazine of professional flight crews published by ALPA, reported events as they occurred but left solidification efforts to Eastern's local ALPA group. Eastern's Master Executive Council chairman Captain Larry Schulte demonstrated some degree of acquiesance when he said (regarding working with Lorenzo): "If he gives us the right flight plan, we'll make sure he gets there."[21]

A second reason for the failure of the resistance may have stemmed from the "legitimate power" held by Eastern's management. Legitimate power "exists when one individual or group is perceived by another as having a sort of charter or social contract, an assigned position, through which that individual or group can exert influence."[22] Legitimate power is held by the establishment in every organization and is a defining characteristic of the establishment. To put it another way, Eastern's establishment had the right to do with it as it pleased because it was the establishment.

In the eyes of much of the traveling and investing public, it was time for Eastern to settle down. The perception of ego-driven bickering between Frank Borman and IAM leader Charlie Bryan had grown tiresome. To many observers, Frank Lorenzo's tough guy tactics were just what the ailing company needed to shape up and fly right. Four months after the sale to Texas Air, Larry Birger, *The Miami Herald* Business/-Monday editor proselytized:

> In 45-year-old Frank Lorenzo, the . . . employees of Eastern Airlines are getting a tough, brilliant, audacious leader who probably understands the intricacies of the business . . . better than any U.S. airline executive . . . . I'm more convinced than

ever of his savvy and management skills . . . .
Eastern will flourish under Lorenzo (emphasis
added). . . . Apart from the IAM problem, I see
relatively smooth sailing for the merger, based on
Lorenzo's word—and I have no reason to doubt
it—that he doesn't intend to try to carve up the
airline.[23]

When resistance efforts failed, the pilots joined the
other unions in requesting a meeting with Lorenzo to discuss the future of the airline. Lorenzo refused to meet
with them. This rejection foreshadowed the stresses and
frustrations of the coming years. The pilots, in defeat,
went back to the business of flying.

Chapter 3, "Relative Peace," discusses a crucial phase
in the destruction of Eastern Airlines, as the pilots and
other employees attempted to adjust to new management.
The interaction between company and employees set a
tone for behaviors that were to persist until the company
folded.

NOTES

1. David Lyons, "Eastern Antagonists Play Out Final
Drama," *The Miami Herald*, January 19, 1987, B7.

2. Larry Birger, "Lorenzo Will be Tough But His
Determination Is What Eastern Needs," *The Miami
Herald*, June 9, 1986, BM5.

3. Captain Don Huckabee, "The Fall of Eastern: Lorenzo's Legacy," *Air Line Pilot* 60 (March 1991): 10.

4. Huckabee, 13.

5. Huckabee, 13.

6. Geoffrey Tomb, "Union Workers Bitter, Worried About Future," *The Miami Herald*, February 25, 1986, A1.

7. Martin Merzer and David Lyons, "Did Eastern Prolong Labor Crisis? Tough Negotiating Tactics May Have Been Used to Impress Buyer," *The Miami Herald*, March 1, 1986, A1.

8. Robert Moorman, "Eastern Gives Leonard Huge Raise; Borman Receives $900,000 Severance," *Air Line Pilot*, 55 (November 1986): 45.

9. David Lyons, "My Gold Parachute Failed, Pilot Says," *The Miami Herald*, August 8, 1986, C5.

10. David Lyons, "Eastern's Labor Chief Expected to Leave," *The Miami Herald*, August 14, 1986, D7.

11. David Lyons, "Eastern's Unions Up the Ante: Offer Concessions and $1.15 Billion," *The Miami Herald*, November 20, 1986, D7.

12.   David Lyons, "EAL Meeting Erupts in Chaos; Merger OK'D," *The Miami Herald*, November 26, 1986, A1.

13.   David Lyons, "Lorenzo Sends Regrets to Labor Leaders," *The Miami Herald*, December 24, 1986, B4.

14.   John Waite Bowers and Donovan Ochs, *The Rhetoric of Agitation and Control* (Reading, Mass.: Addison-Wesley, 1971), 17.

15. Martha Saunders, "Eastern's Employee Communication Crisis," *Public Relations Review* 14 (Summer 1988): 40-41.

16.   Laurel Leff, "Texas Air Chief Not a Hero to All: Tough Tactics Earn Lorenzo Reputation as Union Buster," *The Miami Herald*, February 24, 1986, A8.

17.   Joe Scott, "Our Basic Obligation Is to Run Profitable Airline," *The Falcon*, 25 (March 1986):1.

18.   Lyons, "Lorenzo Sends Regrets," B4.

19.   This information was gathered from a 1987 survey of Eastern pilots conducted by the author.

20.   Moorman, 6.

21.   Moorman, 6.

22.   John Waite Bowers and Donovan Ochs, *The Rhetoric of Agitation and Control* (Reading, Mass.: Addison-Wesley, 1971), 13.

23. Birger, BM5.

3

RELATIVE PEACE

I think everybody's sizing everybody up and
trying to find if there is any way to do
business.
—Jack Bavis, president MEC Council of
ALPA at Eastern[1]

The new year found the pilots of Eastern Airlines back
to the business of flying airplanes. Agitation activities
among the pilots, at least as they were reflected publicly,
dropped off. *The Miami Herald* reported:

Of all the unionized groups, Eastern's 4,500 pilots
are acting the most sanguine, methodically working
to cover all possibilities . . . [They] have kept the

rhetoric down and thoroughly reviewed their options, right down to the day when Eastern might be
integrated into Continental. "I think everybody's
sizing everybody up and trying to find if there is
any way to do business," said Jack Bavis, president
of the Master Executive Council of the Air Line
Pilots Association at Eastern. "We'll listen to what
they have to say and then evaluate it."[2]

TAC, Eastern's new owner, unveiled a business plan
calling for sharp reductions in the number of employees,
deep cuts in wage rates, and the retraining of some
workers for lesser positions. A tough new attendance
policy pricked already tender areas. The policy, imple-
mented in March 1987, stipulated that a pilot would be
disciplined if he or she was absent seven work days
within eighteen months. Pilots protested that the policy
could force flight crew members to fly while sick, a
violation of federal safety rules.[3] Morale plummeted.
After a decade of concessions and bankruptcy threats, the
demoralized employees wondered how much more they
could take. Tension rose to an all-time high.

"It's not necessary, and it's completely stupid in my
opinion," Thomas Peters, the San Francisco-based author
of the best-selling book, *In Search of Excellence*, was
quoted as saying. Although not arguing with the need
for cost controls, Peters said he had spent a great deal of
time speaking to Eastern employees and had found a
level of demoralization unlike any he had ever seen
before.[4]

Among the flight crews, senior pilots continued to take early retirement, while many young pilots left for other carriers.[5] It is important to note here the dilemma of the remaining pilots. Airline pilots earn promotion via a strict seniority policy. That policy exists throughout all ALPA carriers. As a result, an Eastern co-pilot wishing to work for another carrier would have to join that carrier as its most junior second officer [flight engineer]. The consequent loss in pay and status provided a serious deterrent to all but the most junior Eastern pilots and placed many of the remaining pilots' backs squarely against the wall.

Many beseeched ALPA to initiate a national seniority list that would ensure a place, commensurate with experience, for pilots moving from one airline to another, in case their companies folded. The following, quoted from letters to the editor of *Air Line Pilot* are representative:

We need a national seniority list, a national contract, and national professional nonpilot negotiators. We need them today.

—Captain Ray Deeg (Eastern)[6]

A national seniority list may not solve everything, but at least it is unity.

—First Officer George D. Alloway (Eastern)[7]

[Regarding national seniority], are we going to "talk" until it is too late for action, or are we

actively involved in bringing this much-needed effort into being?
—First Officer George M. Moss, Jr. (Eastern)[8]

The notion of modifying the long-standing seniority policy met with mixed response among Eastern's ALPA colleagues. Some favored such a change:

When economic collapse occurs, a nationwide seniority list should be in place to prevent the government and corporations from diluting the power of ALPA. The list should be date of hire first, with adjustments to include prior earnings. This seniority list should be developed and put in place immediately.
—First Officer C.W. Horton (Delta)[9]

Sure wish you would address the very obvious call for a national seniority list . . . . The longer we delay action on these issues, the more difficult it will be to ensure change.
—First Officer William C. Jakeman (Hawaiian)[10]

We need one national seniority list so the various managements can no longer pick us off one at a time.
—Captain J.P. O'Donnell (TWA)[11]

Others did not agree:

When are people . . . going to realize that a national security list isn't going to solve any problems? ALPA is having problems because a number of pilots don't have the guts to stand up for what they believe in. If every ALPA member and every young pilot hoping one day to be in ALPA would not work for a Lorenzo, our way of life could not and would not be changed.

—Captain S. Stanton (Piedmont)[12]

It seems that the advocates [of a national seniority list] are mainly from troubled airlines.

—Captain C.F. Denwalt (Delta)[13]

Hiding behinds cheers of "solidarity," the talk of a national seniority list smacks of preserving jobs of the seniors at the expense of the juniors. I envision someone "senior" to me from a failed airline being hired into a position above me at my airline. Then salt is rubbed in the wounds when the inevitable furlough comes and I get sent to my "alternate" while the "senior new-hire" takes my paycheck home. First right of hire—absolutely! National seniority—no!

—First Officer Rob Briggs (United)[14]

It is useful at this point to delineate the make-up of ALPA. ALPA is a loose confederation of individual unions run by Master Executive Councils (MECs). The MEC of each airline negotiates its own contracts under guidelines issued by ALPA national and is therefore granted a great deal of autonomy. Although final approval of the contracts must come from ALPA national, that organization does not ordinarily become involved in the day-to-day running of the individual unions. The national union does provide financial support during work actions and, as in the case of the Eastern strike, can be influential in ensuring the success or failure of the walkout.[15]

At Eastern, pilot stress increased. A study, conducted at Virginia Polytechnic Institute and State University in cooperation with ALPA, measuring the impact of work events on airline pilots and their families was released in April 1987. Comparisons were made between two pilot groups. Eastern Airlines was chosen to represent a major carrier with a history of unstable management, and USAir and Piedmont were selected to represent carriers with stable managements. The statistics showed that one third of the Eastern pilots and their families showed high levels of stress and that nearly half of them reported an escalation of stress at home. Most (98 percent) were pessimistic about their futures. The report, compiled by Linda Little, a psychologist specializing in occupational stress, concluded that Eastern pilots were "reaching the limits of their coping ability." Eastern officials rejected the study as being invalid because the names for the 420 randomly selected sample were provided by the pilot union.[16]

Individual horror stories of pilot stress were reported in the media:

Captain Ron Russell was being ordered to break the law, and he was frustrated and angry. His bosses at Eastern Airlines, Inc., had instructed him to fly one more trip, even though the Atlanta-to-Houston run would put him over the weekly limit of 30 hours flying time.

Capt. Russell consulted the Federal Aviation Administration, which initially told him to obey regulations. But after an Eastern official contacted the FAA, warning that if the 30-hour rule were rigidly enforced "Eastern could not operate," the agency reversed its decision, according to an FAA memo. Still uneasy, he turned to his union, which warned him not to jeopardize his job.

When Captain Russell finally took off, he was drained from the hours-long dispute. But the twenty-two-year veteran felt even worse when he landed and found that higher FAA officials had slapped him with his first citation ever. It has since been withdrawn and the FAA is investigating the matter.[17]

The conditions at Eastern did not go unnoticed in Washington. In March 1987, the U.S. Senate Subcommittee on Transportation and Related agencies sent the following letter to TAC chairman Frank Lorenzo:

Dear Mr. Lorenzo:

We are writing to express our serious concern over the state of airline service being provided by Texas Air carriers.

In recent months, problems surrounding service on these carriers have reached disturbing levels. Frequent fliers have become frequent losers. Lost time, lost money, and lost baggage have become all too common for passengers on Continental and other Texas Air flights. Now, passengers are losing patience.

When the Congress passed the Airline Deregulation Act in 1978, it was with the intention of providing the travelling public with more affordable, efficient air carrier service through enhanced competition. To a large extent, that goal has been achieved. Deregulation of the airline industry has made air travel accessible to millions who otherwise would never have flown. Commutation by air is not only possible, but practical for a diverse group of travellers, if the service is reliable.

A number of small, independent carriers flourished under a deregulated air carrier system. However, recently a number of these carriers, such as People Express, have been acquired by larger carriers. In the last fifteen months, twenty-five major mergers have taken place in the airline industry. Texas Air has participated in this process, acquiring Eastern,

New York Air, People Express and Frontier. A number of small commuter airlines have also been acquired by Texas Air. The result has been diminished levels of service.

Since Continental purchased People Express and New York Air, severe problems exist throughout the system. Excessive delays, overbooking, unexplained cancellations and poor communications at the terminals and in the planes have become commonplace. Crews and ground personnel appear to lack adequate training and resources. Equipment problems are evidently a serious part of the troubles and raise concerns and fears about safety.

In expanding its air carrier network, Texas Air appears to have forgotten its passengers. Constituent complaints to our offices regarding problems encountered using Continental have increased significantly.

Texas Air decisions affecting employees of its acquired airlines have led to serious problems within the workforce. The stress that air crews, including pilots, are being put under has harmed employee morale and the level of service. There is cause for concern over the impact these problems could have on safety.[Emphasis added]

Deregulation presented tremendous opportunities for

both the aviation industry and its passengers. However, the abuse of those opportunities by the industry, through its seeming disregard for adequate service, is inviting reregulation of the airline industry.

We do not endorse reregulation. It would represent a step backward in efforts to promote air service through a competitive marketplace. However, satisfactory resolution of the problems facing air travellers is needed as quickly as possible.

We request that you provide us with a report on the problems being experienced with Texas Air carriers, and what steps you are taking to address those issues. Specifically, we would like you to address: the increased number of flight cancellations, many of them unexplained; flight delays; overbookings; lost or delayed baggage; crew tardiness; deteriorated service, including lack of food on flights; and morale problems among employees of acquired airlines.

Texas Air utilizes a scarce resource—the flight lanes and landing slots at our nation's busy airports. Texas Air has an obligation to provide a reasonable level of service to its passengers. Currently, that obligation is not being met. As members of the Senate with jurisdiction over aviation issues, we have a responsibility to our constituents to ensure that reliable, affordable air service is available to them. We urge you to work toward that goal.

We look forward to a prompt response.

Sincerely,
Lowell P. Weicker, Jr.
Frank R. Lautenberg, Chairman

Pilots began to complain that Eastern's cost-cutting policies were creating unsafe flying conditions. In response, the Federal Aviation Administration (FAA) increased safety inspections at Eastern. The pilots launched a write-in campaign aimed at getting Congress to investigate safety issues in the airline industry in June, two months after they had picketed ten airports nationwide to draw attention to the safety issue. They charged that belt-tightening was compromising safety at Eastern and cited episodes in which Eastern planes flew with unsafe equipment. To these charges the company responded that ALPA's "so-called safety campaign" was really nothing more than a ploy to cover up the union's real concern—"preservation of $100,000 a year salaries for only 55 hours of flying per month."[18]

By October, the safety issue had prompted a Congressional hearing at which pilots told Congress of incidents of coercion by the carrier to fly unsafe planes. In December, an event in Pensacola, Florida, served to support the pilots' complaints. An accident occurred involving an Eastern jet that cracked in half while landing.[19] The event, among others, served to fuel pilot protests into the coming year.

Meanwhile, a suit, filed by ALPA in federal court in Washington, sought to stop the company from transferring aircraft and other assets to nonunion subsidiaries of TAC. The airline posted a $67.4 million loss for the third quarter, prompting additional expense cuts and layoffs.[20]   By the end of the year, the pilots were threatening a strike vote and legal action in response to the carrier's alleged plans to sell its profitable Northeast corridor shuttle.

COMMUNICATION STRATEGIES OF PILOTS AND MANAGEMENT

Pilot Responses

On the surface, agitation activities among the pilots were relatively subdued during the first part of 1987. The pilots, in their attempts to come to terms with the new management, went "back to the drawing board," as activities that involved the milder agitative strategies of petition, promulgation, and polarization. The pilots, submissive after Frank Lorenzo's victory in securing the airline, retreated to typical lines of communication, such as talks, letters, and "normal" forms of discourse. The first six months of the year were quiet.   Later in the year, promulgation activities included ad campaigns surrounding the safety issue and letters to congressmen. The flag issue of safety drew a great deal of media attention, but events *not* covered in the news may have contributed most profoundly to the pilots' behavior in the coming years.

The agitation strategy of solidification, which had been only weakly evident during The Resistance, was gaining strength. As an indicator of this, a pilots' union newsletter, *Eastern Pilot's Checklist*, began publication around mid-year in an atttempt to galvanize pilots' emotions. In the June 19 issue, Eastern's MEC chairman Jack Bavis, Jr., addressed a shaky constituency when he wrote:

I am struggling to find a way to resolve all of our problems in a timely and equitable way. I have heard those of you who wish to take a labor action now. I have heard those of you who are voting with your feet [referring to the growing number of pilots leaving the company]. I have also heard those of you who are uncertain and want to believe that we can resolve our differences if we would only meet and bargain with management[21]

The publication invited pilots and their spouses to express their feelings and provided one of the few forums for pilot input throughout the crisis. Each issue included a family awareness column designed to keep up the spirit on the home front. This inclusion of pilots' families was to continue throughout the upcoming crisis. The November 1987 issue included an open letter to Eastern pilots and their spouses from a concerned pilot's wife: "If family awareness and communications committees are not geared up pretty soon, we'll all be goners in our attempts to salvage EAL and keep Frank Lorenzo from selling us way, way short!"[22]

The slick, sixteen-page newsletter contained emotion-laden headlines. One headline, "It's Not Over 'til It's Over," borrowed the often quoted Yogi Berra line to introduce an editorial encouraging the pilots to gear up for the "long haul," and to make some effort toward overcoming any ill-feelings (a tradition among the generally conservative pilots) toward the other employee groups. The article concluded with the following caution:

> We, the pilot group, aren't alone in this attempt to preserve a rewarding and stable career here at Eastern Airlines. The other employee groups are sharing the same abuse and stress that we are. Let's remember that we're all on the same team. Let's continue to treat each other with the courtesy, respect and professional good will that we would like to have shown to us.[23]

"The Bottom of the Morality Barrel," heralded an article critical of Eastern's employee publication, *The Falcon*, which had published an account of a pilot from another airline who had been fired for reporting to work drunk, but whose job was being fought for by ALPA. This attempt to discredit ALPA outraged the pilots who pointed to the Human Intervention and Motivation System Guidelines that had been violated in the firings. The article concluded, "If management has to go that far back in history (1982) and sink that far down the morality barrel to find something with which to slander ALPA regarding safety, we must be doing something right. Keep up the good work."[24]

"Expect the worst . . . Hope for the Best," in the November 1987 issue, headlined an editorial calling Lorenzo "an absentee landlord who has bought into a viable operation, looted it, and then blamed the tenants for the slum-like condition he created," reinforcing Lorenzo as a flag individual in their polarization efforts.

Increases in the agitative strategy of promulgation were evident at this time. An appeal for involvement in media relations appeared in the June issue. Pilots and their families were urged to become involved to help develop media contacts and to track down and document events, rumors, and stories of interest.[25]

Management's Responses

Eastern's management continued to maintain avoidance tactics during 1987, primarily in the form of counter-persuasion (i.e., taking under advisement, rebuttals) and evasion (i.e., refusal to comment). In addition, the company followed avoidance tactics that included seeking public support, accusations, laying blame, and taking legal action. The question of whether or not the company employed suppressive tactics arises in light of the firings that took place. Indeed, firings occurred, and industry observers noted their impact on morale. Whether these terminations were *intended* to be suppressive is beyond the scope of this study. The fact remains that they did occur, and they occurred at a time when new management was "taking charge." Even if not intentionally suppressive, these firings should not be overlooked as having a profound impact on the morale of the pilots and other employees.

The Falcon continued counterpersuasive tactics by focusing strongly on management's emphasis on profit and cost reduction. The publication addressed management's stringent new absenteeism policy (without any reference to the pilots as a unique employee group) in its March 11, 1987, issue as follows:

> When an airline pays out nearly $80 million in one year to cover absenteeism, something is amiss. Yet that's what Eastern was forced to spend throughout 1986 because of absenteeism.

> And the corporation paid much of that sum to people who were absent from their work stations for reasons other than illness, thereby placing an unfair burden on their fellow employees and on managers who had to juggle personnel to cover for their being away from the job.[26]

In May, *The Falcon* returned fire on the safety issue in an article titled "On ALPA and safety." In an apparent attempt to discredit ALPA as a proponent of airline safety, the article pointed to the incident mentioned earlier in which a pilot for Northwest Airlines was fired for flying drunk.   A previous *Falcon* story (April 29) described ALPA's support of a Delta Airlines pilot allegedly drunk on the job.[27]   This response outraged the pilots who felt the company was dredging up remote incidents in order to discredit ALPA's efforts toward promoting safety, but it may have been useful in influencing employees who were not decided on where they stood with this issue.

About mid-year, *Falcon* headlines moved toward a more promotional orientation. "Accepting the Eastern Challenge," reflected an interview with Eastern's vice president of human resources, Tom Matthews, who argued, "Eastern's historical failure to earn a consistent profit has been the backdrop to periods of hostility between management and some employee unions . . . . The best thing management can do to help employees is to structure the company to "earn a consistent rate of return."[28]

In October, the publication featured "Eastern Today," in which President Phil Bakes commented, "Eastern is in a less strong position than it was a year ago . . . . We have not made any significant progress on one of our basic problems and that is a cost structure we can't live with."[29]

Letters to the editor began to include letters from passengers and others who were offended by "pilot propaganda" and employee complaints. An example from the August issue follows:

I am a Frequent Traveler and Executive Traveler with

Eastern. However, I was incensed to discover a stack of the enclosed brochures in the first class lavatory [referring to handouts distributed by ALPA-represented pilots during their picketing].

Regardless of the pilot's union views, the traveling public should not be subjected to this propaganda on the planes.[30]

Anti-pilot, anti-union sentiments emerged at this time in the form of articles like "Eastern Pilot Picketing Drives Customers to Other Airlines, Ignores Competitive Marketplace, Slows Company's Progress."[31] In November, possibly in response to *The Eastern Pilot's Checklist*, an unnamed newsletter was submitted to the pilots from Eastern's flight operations. In the first issue, chief pilot Don Breeding promised, "You will never see any politically motivated articles in our newsletter. It is intended to be and will be a means to make you aware of significant happenings in Flight Operations and closely related areas in the Company." The newsletter went on to include the slogan, "The Things That Contribute Most to Safety and Cost Nothing Are Attitudes!"

CONCLUSIONS

A trendline tracing the pilot agitative activities as reflected in the news media is included in Chapter 7. The diagram indicates a low level of agitation during 1987—at least as it was evident to the general public.

The apparent calmness of the year is deceiving, however, as the most significant communication activities of the crisis may well have taken place during this time of relative peace.

By this time, all of the pilots who could have bailed out had done so, leaving those remaining with few choices. From a theoretical perspective, actual and potential membership of the agitative group was increasing, primarily as a result of the flag issue of safety. One pilot reflected on the issue in his response to a 1987 survey: "I'm not a member of ALPA, but I'm with my fellow pilots all the way. Why you ask? Because the son-of-a-bitch [Lorenzo] is trying to kill me!"[32] (This remark appeared among responses to a 1987 survey of pilot communication needs, conducted by the author).

The 1987 survey concluded, among other things, that the pilots shared strong perceptions of crisis. In spite of high levels of perceived constraint, they continued to communicate actively—perhaps even avidly. They sought information from a variety of sources but trusted relatively few. They were suspicious of mass media reports because they feared the company's advertising dollar could "buy" favorable coverage.

Careful attention to solidification strategies, most notably through the *The Eastern Pilot's Checklist* and Family Awareness programs, laid a strong, cohesive foundation, which was to serve the Eastern pilots well over the coming months. Their level of rhetorical sophistication became apparent as the pilots developed media relations committees, produced the *Checklist*, and organized telephone "tree" communications systems.[33]

The company's tough posture precluded any adjustment behavior and contributed to the pilots' sense of powerlessness. Although well-equipped rhetorically, there is evidence that corporate communicators were restricted from doing their jobs in ways they thought best. Management's credibility was poor and its power was eroding.[34]

These combinations contributed to the rebellion of 1988 and subsequently to the walkout.   Chapter 4 discusses the pilots' activities as they passed a point of no return in their efforts to unseat what they perceived as unacceptable management.

NOTES

1. David Lyons, "Eastern Antagonists Play Out Final Drama," *The Miami Herald*, January 19, 1987, B7.

2. Lyons, "Eastern Antagonists," B7.

3.   David Lyons, "Eastern Pilots Rap Sick Rules; Management Says It's Curbing Abuse," *The Miami Herald*, January 28, 1987, B5.

4.   David Lyons, "Eastern Workers Feel the Iron Fist," *The Miami Herald*, March 29, 1987, C1.

5. David Lyons, "More Eastern Pilots Bailing Out," *The Miami Herald*, March 10, 1987, B5.

6. "Pilots' Forum," *Air Line Pilot* 55 (October 1986): 2.

7. "Pilots' Forum," *Air Line Pilot* 55 (November 1986): 2.

8. "Pilots' Forum," *Air Line Pilot* 55 (November 1986): 2.

9. "Pilots' Forum," *Air Line Pilot* 55 (September 1986): 56.

10. "Pilots' Forum," *Air Line Pilot* 55 (September 1986): 56.

11. "Pilots' Forum," *Air Line Pilot* 55 (September 1986): 56.

12. "Pilots' Forum," *Air Line Pilot* 55 (September 1986): 56.

13. "Pilots' Forum," *Air Line Pilot* 55 (November 1986): 2.

14. "Pilots' Forum," *Air Line Pilot* 55 (November 1986): 2.

15. Jerry Jackson, Eastern MEC Communications chairman, telephone interview by author, March 11, 1988.

16. Jackson interview.

17. Paulette Thomas, "Bumpy Ride: Pilots Feel the Stress of Turmoil in the Airline Industry," *The Wall Street Journal*, April 24, 1987, 3(1).

18. David Satterfield, "Eastern Pilots to Deluge D.C. with Postcards," *The Miami Herald*, June 11, 1987, C6.

19. Frank Cerabino, "Eastern Jet Cracks Open On Landing In Pensacola," *The Miami Herald*, December 29, 1987, A1.

20. David Lyons, "Eastern to Layoff 3,000," *The Miami Herald*, November 11, 1987, A1.

21. Captain J.J. Bavis, Jr., "Master Chairman's Report," *Eastern Pilot's Checklist*, June 19, 1987, 2.

22. "An Open Letter to Eastern Pilots and Their Spouses From a Concerned Pilot's Wife," *Eastern Pilot's Checklist*, November 1987, 2.

23. "It's Not Over 'Til It's Over," *Eastern Pilot's Checklist*, June 19, 1987, 1.

24. Captain Bob Breslin, "The Bottom of the Morality Barrel," *Eastern Pilot's Checklist*, June 19, 1987, 16.

25. "Your Media Relations Committee Needs Your

Help," *Eastern Pilot's Checklist*, June 19, 1987, 16.

26.   "New EAL Attendance Program Stemming Absenteeism Rates," *The Falcon*, 26 (March 11, 1987): 1.

27. "ALPA Safety Concerns at Delta," *The Falcon*, 26 (April 29, 1987): 2.

28. "Accepting the Eastern Challenge," *The Falcon*, 26 (August 1987): 1.

29. "Eastern Today," *The Falcon*, 26 (October 1987): 1.

30. "Service Outstanding But Pilot Propaganda Is Bad News," *The Falcon*, 26 (August 1987): 2.

31.   "Eastern Pilot Picketing Drives Customers to Other Airlines, Ignores Competitive Marketplace, Slows Company's Progress," *The Falcon*, 26 (April 29, 1987): 2.

32. Results of the survey were published in *Public Relations Review* 14 (Summer 1988): 33-44.

33.   A telephone tree communication system was outlined for the pilots in an April 21, 1987, letter from Jerry Jackson, chairman, MEC Communications.

34. Martha Saunders, "Eastern's Employee Communication Crisis," *Public Relations Review* 14 (Summer 1988): 38.

4

THE REBELLION

Q. What if the pilots don't come to work
—who will fly?

A. I don't think that will happen.
—Chief Pilot's Message, March 1,
1989[1]

By 1988, the pilots were "mad as hell." Much of their distress stemmed from two issues: (1) the company's hiring of a small airline to operate flights in the event of a strike by the IAM and (2) the proposed sale of the popular and profitable Northeast shuttle to a new unit of TAC.

Shifting quickly into escalation/confrontation, the unionized pilots threatened to stage a nationwide walkout or some other job action if the company allowed the small carrier Orion Air to operate Eastern routes. Labor officials claimed that such a deal with Orion Air would be a direct violation of their contracts, "which gives members the exclusive right to perform work at the airline." ALPA chairman Henry Duffy protested: "Pilots all over the United States will see this as a threat to the profession . . . . If one company could get away with this, other companies with like minds could duplicate it." [2]

Weeks later, after first refusing comment, the company confirmed that it had made the deal with Orion because the pilots' union refused to provide assurances that its members would fly through a machinists' strike.[3] The pilots' concerns, at least as they involved the company's plan for a "back-up airline," were put to rest when U.S. District Judge Barrington O. Parker ruled that Eastern could not use non-Eastern pilots as a means of undermining ALPA's status as the exclusive collective bargaining representative for the airline pilots employed by Eastern.[4]

A broad publicity campaign, designed to blast Frank Lorenzo, brought the chairman of Texas Air into full focus as a flag individual; bumper stickers appeared in Miami saying, "Lorenzo Gives Greed a Bad Name." The safety issue raged on, as two events in Florida served to further the pilots' polarization efforts. In Miami, pieces of a burning engine from an Eastern plane fell on a used-car storage lot and started a grass fire.[5] An accident in Pensacola involving an Eastern jet, which had cracked in half while landing, remained unexplained.[6] In April, the

FAA fined the company $823,500 for another round of safety violations and began a thirty-day inspection of Eastern's entire fleet. The U.S. Department of Transportation announced an unprecedented probe into the finances and managerial competence of TAC, citing concern over recurring safety problems. In June, the issue lost power when the FAA pronounced the airline, "fit to fly"—a move that prompted protest from the pilots. In a report by the Department of Transportation and the FAA, Eastern was declared to meet industry safety standards and have only the usual maintenance lapses. The pilots blasted the report and accused Transportation Secretary James Burnley of glossing over significant problems. An ALPA response to the report follows:

> Our preliminary analysis of the . . . report shows that the FAA found significant problems at Eastern which had been identified by Eastern pilots previous to the investigation, but which were either glossed over, ignored or buried by Mr. Burnley when he gave his interpretation of the report."[7]

ALPA attempted to reopen the issue in February when it filed a petition charging the (then) former secretary of transportation with violation of federal conflict of interest laws and asking the Department of Transportation to vacate Burnley's ruling in favor of Eastern and against ALPA. It seemed that at the same time Burnley had issued the ruling, he was negotiating employment with two law firms that had substantial links to Eastern. In addition, ALPA questioned whether the tone of Burnley's "unprecedented vituperative and false attacks against ALPA" might have been set by a desire to impress a prospective employer. Burnley had, in fact, been hired by the Washington, D.C., law firm of Shaw, Pittman, Potts & Trowbridge; had become a partner in the firm; and was to do work for Eastern and Continental. ALPA argued:

> To anyone who has followed Texas Air Corp. strategy, this episode shouldn't offer any surprises; over the past decade, TAC has raised the seamy act of influence peddling to the status of high art. They have arrogantly demonstrated what can be accomplished by powerful men with big money and seemingly limitless influence who crave a goal for which they are willing to stretch, suspend, or wink at ethics and the law.[8]

Texas Air cancelled its proposed purchase of the Northeast shuttle, but within months, the company announced a tentative deal to sell the shuttle to real estate mogul Donald Trump. The unions sued to block the deal, but in December 1988, Judge Parker approved the sale, and the "pride of the fleet" was excised, in spite of Frank Lorenzo's 1986 promise of having no intention to downsize the airline.

By the end of 1988, much of the public was fed up with the bickering between Eastern's management and labor—especially in light of perceived IAM antics. An editorial in *The Miami Herald* protested:

Anyone who ever doubted what havoc spoiled brats can wreak when fighting for control of a business need only look at Eastern Airlines. Both management and union leaders seem to delight at plucking the feathers out of Eastern's once-mighty wings and holding them up for the world to admire. Neither seems to have noticed a public aghast at this inch-meal destruction.

Why have Eastern's troubles turned into such charades? Because after months of threats, work slowdowns, asset shuffles, Federal safety inspections, and lawsuits, the individuals involved seem to have lost all sight of their objectives. Pettiness rules.

It's truly tragic to see Eastern's "Wings of Man," once so nobly silhouetted outstretched against the sky, folding inexorably . . . into a shroud.[9]

Subsequent articles revealed growing impatience with the situation at Eastern. Travel agent Nilda Rinehart was quoted in *The Miami Herald*: "Passengers call me and the first thing they tell me is, 'Don't book me on Eastern.'"[10]

Meanwhile, the IAM was moving closer to a strike. In February 1989, the company rejected a government offer to settle the dispute through arbitration, an act that set the stage for a thirty-day cooling-off period. This "cooling-off period" turned into the beleaguered airline's final showdown.

The big question in the media at the time was whether the pilots would back an IAM strike. The pilots' union, in an effort to push management into a quick contract agreement, urged its 3,400 members to consider supporting a possible strike—a distasteful prospect for many of the pilots who resented the recalcitrant behavior of the IAM in the past. This issue was a critical one to the company, as the pilots' participation would certainly be a devastating blow to the company; however, management did not believe the pilots would really walk. Company officials assured Wall Street and travel agents that the animosity between the two unions was so intense "that the pilots would gladly keep the airline flying if the IAM walked off the job on March 4."[11]

Unfortunately, management's evaluation was wrong in two respects: it neglected to consider the pilots' hatred for Frank Lorenzo, and it underestimated the solidarity among the ranks of pilots. This miscalculation is understandable error, since the pilots had never before shown such an intense dislike for management that they would side with the IAM. However, on February 15, in a rare recommendation, the pilots' union leaders at Eastern Airlines formally urged their members to stay home if the IAM were to go on strike. The National Mediation Board (NMB) recommended that President Bush intervene in order to avert the strike, but the president refused to do so. Last minute contract talks between the pilots and management ended with no agreement, and on

March 4, the machinists' strike began. Most of Eastern's 4,200 pilots walked out in sympathy.

COMMUNICATION STRATEGIES OF PILOTS AND MANAGEMENT

Pilot Responses

The pilots maintained strong petitioning, solidification, and polarization activities throughout this period. As the situation deteriorated, toward the end of 1988, they moved into escalation/confrontation mode but were unable to move the company toward adjustment.

Petitioning activities continued, as pilot leaders met with representatives of Trans World Airlines chairman Carl Icahn to discuss a possible buyout of the Miami-based carrier. Meetings resumed between management and the pilots on a job security-for-concessions plan.

Solidification tactics were intensified to reinforce pilots' ideology, and lift spirits. A videotape was released featuring Charles Plumb, a former U.S. Navy pilot who was shot down over North Vietnam. In a powerful emotional appeal, Plumb spoke to Eastern's pilots about how he survived 2,103 days in a prison camp and prescribed how they could "counter the negative atmosphere" at Eastern.[12]

Eastern Pilot's Checklist continued to pump up the troops. In February, an editorial accused Eastern's management of manufacturing the current crisis in order to extract massive concessions from the employees. The editorial continued by revealing the existence of "hard evidence" emerging from "the Company's own documents supporting the claim."

> An analysis of those documents reveals that Eastern, if it didn't have the burden of Texas Air dragging it down, would have made $80 million last year instead of the $180 million dollar loss reported by management—a $260 million dollar swing. As we have said on other occasions, the Eastern employees do, indeed, make a profit for the company, and have for many years. The problem is that those profits always get picked up elsewhere before they make it to our bottom line. Labor costs aren't out of line at Eastern, but our management is.[13]

The pilots found encouragement in the public support their activities were inspiring, as their promulgation efforts took root. The April *Checklist* featured a reprint of a letter from Harvard economics professor Lawrence H. Summers, which had originally appeared in *The Boston Globe*. The letter, addressed to Phillip Bakes, president of Eastern Airlines, accused the company's management of "cut and run" mentality:

> Cutting and running, I conjecture, is the essence of your strategy. This explains why you have separated your profitable air shuttle service from the remainder of your airline; why you so vigorously promote your ONE PASS program with its promise of free flights in the future; and why you do not

take the steps necessary to improve service quality. Your intention of cutting and running may also explain why Texas Air has invested much more heavily in improving and advertising Continental's service quality than in upgrading Eastern's perform-ance.[14]

The promulgation tactic of a full page ad in *USA Today* brought favorable response from the general public. The ad attacked parts of a letter written by Phil Bakes to everyone enrolled in the company's frequent flier program. According to the ad, Bakes's letter contained many factual errors as well as glaring omis-sions, "which serve to present a biased view of the current state of affairs at our airline." The pilots' ad continued by submitting information as to Eastern's prof-itability, service, and safety. Subsequent letters from the public were printed in *Checklist*. For example:

I firmly believe that through informative advertise-ments such as yours the public will finally begin to believe how horrible major companies such as Eastern will treat their employees. I cannot tell you how many people are sympathetic to the pilots of Eastern for having to suffer such mental abuse.

There are always two sides in a disagreement and unfortunately yours has not been told until now.

So, please consider this as a statement of support

for your position. As we, the passengers, depend
on the pilot's good judgement to ensure our safety,
it is reassuring to me that you have had the courage
to take the stand that you have. I only wish the
FAA had the same courage.

I am in your debt and my gratitude is yours—Keep
up the excellent fight, my prayers and best hopes
are with each of you.[15]

The escalation/confrontation tactic of nonverbal
offensive emerged as the pilots began wearing copper
"Eastern Held Hostage" bracelets. In response to firings
of pilots who refused to take out airplanes they deemed
unsafe, the MEC had created the Hostage Fund in order
to provide some income to those pilots who had been
disciplined and were awaiting hearings.   Through a
voluntary assessment of $1 a day, each donor was given
a bracelet which would serve to remind management of
pilot solidarity.[16]

MEC chairman Jack Bavis urged unity. In his April
report, entitled "Tolerance," he admonished his constituency "to be tolerant and respectful of the opinions of
others within the pilot group during these times of stress
and uncertainty." Bavis continued:

I am reiterating that message at this time because of
the hardening of attitude that I see within the pilot
group to the unrelenting demands of management.

Our solidarity sends a clear signal to the company that we are not to be trifled with and must be dealt with fairly.   Unfortunately, that same solidarity produces a dangerous by-product—an insensitivity to those among us who dissent from the course chosen by fellow pilots. . . . We are all after the same goal. . . . Your MEC is not a rubber stamp as to the best way to achieve those goals. It debates —sometimes heatedly—it deliberates, and it reaches a consensus. It does not stifle the opinion of others, it fosters it.   Only in that way can all sides be heard. I suggest that each of us might do well to do likewise. The "enemy" is not within our ranks, but without. Let's stand united.[17]

Bavis's struggle with the more radical elements within the pilot ranks was to endure into the strike, when a more aggressive strike committee gained power. The "opinions of others" defended by Bavis included members of a group of pilots calling themselves "Pilots With Another View," who had sent letters to their fellow pilots pleading for moderation:

We the undersigned are in agreement, there is another view of Eastern. A more positive and dynamic view than what is portrayed. Quite frankly we're tired of all the bashing and negative talk about our family. We believe a more moderate voice, indeed the majority voice, is not being heard clearly. We believe, by making our voices heard,

we *can* make a positive impact on behalf of all the
pilots. We believe a majority of Eastern Pilots do
not want to buy the airline, take further pay cuts,
pledge any part of their retirement, become business
partners with the IAM, or join hands with the IAM
in negotiations. . . . We are not against *ALPA*! We
are not against *MANAGEMENT*! We are *FOR
EASTERN*! [18]

The letter was unsigned but printed names of ninety-
seven organizers and supporters of "Pilots With Another
View," many of whom were supervisory pilots. Mailing
labels had been provided by the company. Many of the
pilots were incensed at the breach in their unity. The
Checklist provided a forum for their responses:

[To] Steve Glasgow, Organizer of Pilots With
Another View:
Dear Steve:
You must have irrefutable proof of a complete
reversal in the very character in Frank Lorenzo and
his paid henchmen or you surely would not risk the
best chance we have of loosing the strangle hold
these unconscionable people have on us and our
loved ones.

[To] Eastern's president, Phil Bakes
Dear Mr. Bakes:
Today I received a letter from a group called the
"Pilots With Another View." I am not writing you

about the contents of this letter, but, rather how they obtained my name and home address. Mr. Steve Glasgow, one of the organizers of this group, informed me that Eastern Airlines has sold the pilot mailing labels to his group. Is this possible? How could Eastern Airlines jeopardize the safety and security of my home and family by making public this information for any would-be bandit or terrorist to use as he/she saw fit? I will hold you personally responsible if, because of your actions, any harm comes to my family.[19]

It is difficult to determine what was going on in the minds of "Pilots With Another View," since they did not have available to them the powerful forum provided by the *Checklist*. However, a glimpse into their collective psyche may be reflected in the following terse letter of resignation from ALPA (written on Eastern Airlines letterhead) which was printed and responded to in the June 1988 *Checklist*:

April 14, 1988

Membership Service—Eastern Airlines
Air Line Pilots Association
535 Herndon Parkway
Herndon, VA 22070

Please consider this letter my resignation from ALPA effective immediately.

Please inform me of dues owed under Executive Inactive status.

I regret the necessity for this step, but it has become clear that ALPA is willing to sacrifice Eastern Airlines to topple Texas Air and in good conscience I can no longer tolerate the position and direction of the Association.

B. Stephens
Staff Vice President—Flying[20]

The letter suggests, as do the few available comments from other pilots with similar views, that some of the pilots believed ALPA to be waging its furious battle in order to protect the *union*, not the airline. To them, the unrelenting demands by ALPA were unacceptable. Pat Lee, who was active with Pilots With Another View during its original organization, but who withdrew later in the year wrote:

The goals we established at the time were honorable and, in my opinion, in line with the general thinking of the line pilots of Eastern. The original goals were

1. no B fund to buy EAL
2. total disassociation with or from the IAM
3. realistic goals for a contract given the horrible situation we found ourselves in.

We were to be a lobbying effort with ALPA to ensure they were aware of how most of the line pilots felt. We, quite frankly, felt the general feeling by certain factions on the MEC was not in line with the feeling of the line pilots in general. As you know, we attended union meetings and lobbied for our position. The situation, however, changed in early June and PWAV, in my opinion became the voice of management.[21]

By May 1988, even Bavis's patience with the dissidents had been stretched. In the *Checklist* editorial that month he wrote:

It is one thing to have a disagreement with fellow pilots over the problems we are facing and the solutions to those problems. It is quite another to carry that disagreement outside of the pilot group and actively campaign against those who are trying to do the job the membership has endorsed. . . . Our handful willfully collaborate by parroting the company line in the halls of Congress. They willfully collaborate by participating in staged press conferences to mouth prepared party line statements. They willfully collaborate by rumor-mongering against their fellow pilots in order to sow seeds of suspicions. . . . But it is hard to believe that The Collaborators ever go through a night without feeling a cold sweat break out with the realization they have broken faith with their comrades in arms.[22]

By early fall, the pilots' fury had seemingly taken on a life of its own; there could be little doubt as to where they were headed. The *Checklist* produced frenzied letters from pilots and their wives, as well as reprints of magazine and newspaper articles sympathetic with the pilots.[23] An article reprinted from *Business Month Magazine* suggested "Frank Lorenzo built the world's biggest airline company on reckless price cutting, government aid and lots of debt. He will need a miracle to keep it flying."[24]

In some instances, the attacks seemed juvenile, as in the case of the "Texas Air Management Aptitude Test," published in *Checklist* in September. The "test" included nine absurdly simple questions and was introduced as follows:

> This is the same test given to Bakes, Breeding, Matthews and other senior management types. These questions are exceedingly difficult and may require many hours of deep thought on your part. 6 correct answers entitle you to a Texas Air Management job interview. 3 correct answers entitle you to replace Phil Bakes as President of Eastern. So, sharpen those pencils, and good luck.[25]

The pages of the *Checklist* revealed, in its letters and articles, a somber awareness of the inevitable. In some cases, the pilots indicated a steeled acceptance of whatever would be. One wrote:

> What this comes down to, bottom line, is that this company is part of me; the people I fly with are in a very real sense, my family. I know more about some of my second officers' lives than I know about my Aunt Francis from Pasadena. I was here when the last Connie retired and when Colonel Frank was considered a good guy by some, and one of us by others. Like many of my classmates, I shuttled on the Electra and suffered through the furloughs, celebrated the award of new routes and mourned when Captain Eddie died. . . . I'm locked in here for a number of reasons, not the least of which is that I just hate to see a bully win. The Lorenzos of this world are bullies; they try to throw their weight around and control or intimidate the other guy until enough people stand up and say "Enough already!" . . . . The black and gold uniform I currently own will probably be the only airline uniform I will ever wear. I do not intend to chase another flying job if by some outside change, the people at Texas Air manage to bring us down. I have made my decision to stand and fight.[26]

The writing was on the wall when the January 1989 issue of *Eastern Pilot's Checklist* appeared. The machinists were entering a mandated thirty-day cooling off period, and pilot leaders were urging the pilots to consider supporting a possible IAM strike. Their beloved shuttle was being sold. The safety issue, still unresolved, had lost its impact. Pilot representatives remained in talks with management over contract issues that could decide whether or not the pilots would cross the picket lines; yet, the *Checklist* was filled with grim strike preparation information. Included in this issue was an essay, "I Believe in Prayer," written by Captain Eddie Rickenbacker in 1945, in which the spiritual leader of Eastern Airlines advised, "The easiest thing in the world is to die; the hardest is to live. . . . I humbly think man instinctively does not interest himself in others. He does it by an act of will." [27]

The *Checklist* employed powerful emotional appeals. An article in the February-March 1988 issue, running with the taunting headline "Are Pilots Wimps?" asked, "Can it be true that these same men and women who flew in Vietnam and Korea, fly in all kinds of inclement weather, and subject themselves to physical and mental scrutiny throughout their careers, do not really have the 'Right Stuff'?"[28]

War metaphors emerged, an effective persuasive tactic for the pilots, many of whom had obtained their flight training in preparation for combat flying during the Vietnam and Korean conflicts. The same issue of *Checklist* included a letter of resignation from Eastern pilot Ronald Hoffmeyer and was titled "Another of Our Wounded Pauses to Say Goodbye."[29] ALPA's strike contingency fund was referred to as its "war chest." In other issues, the words of George Washington, Patrick Henry, Ben Franklin, and The Holy Bible were invoked to stir the pilots to band together and fight tyranny. One especially interesting anecdote involved Jacques Cousteau telling how a school of dolphins can kill a shark (Lorenzo was often referred to as a "shark" by the pilots and media). Cousteau described the occasion:

Nature itself offers us inspiration about the power of numbers. A large shark purposefully circles a school of dolphins. Waiting. . . waiting. . . waiting. The dolphins sense the danger. And they work together to fend off the aggressor. The dolphins turn at once, suddenly, as if they were one! They dive beneath the shark, then hurtle upwards, driving their blunt noses into the shark's belly, one after another. It is the perfect strategy! With no ribs to protect its vital organs, the shark is vulnerable. For all of its power, it is defeated by intelligence and the sheer force of numbers.[30]

The May 1988 issue of *Checklist* provided a chilling comparison of pilots who had transported Orion planes and crew to Miami (where they were to serve management's strike preparation efforts) to Judas Iscariot, who had betrayed his Master for thirty pieces of silver. An additional allusion, this one to Nazi Germany, contributed to the pilots' polarization efforts when it asked of these fellow pilots: "What will they do when they are asked to 'eat their own?'" The article closed with the following warning: "Judas when he realized what he had done, went out and hung himself. Think about it the next time one of the 'high priests' of Texas Air offers you thirty pieces of silver."[31]

Eastern's pilots enjoyed the support of their colleagues from other airlines as they moved toward a standoff with Frank Lorenzo. *Air Line Pilot* included numerous letters of support throughout 1988 and early 1989:

> Those of us who think "Eastern's problems don't affect me" are engaging in wishful thinking.
> —Second Officer Patrick S. Palazzolo (United)[32]

> In spite of all our troubles here at Northwest, I feel fortunate compared to what the Eastern guys are going through.
> —First Officer Charles Brantley (Republic)[33]

> It is time for a nationwide shutdown! We cannot let Eastern Airlines quietly slip away.
> —Second Officer John Flanders (United)[34]

> Lorenzo has crossed the line! What he has done at Eastern Airlines is criminal.
> —First Officer Robert P. Gick (Pan Am)[35]

It would be irresponsible to end any coverage of Eastern's pilot rebellion without at least a mention of the role of Farrell Kupersmith, associate managing partner of Touche Ross, ALPA's financial consultant. It was Kupersmith who encouraged the pilots to enter the strike through his assurances that Lorenzo would be forced to sell the airline. In a video distributed to the pilots immediately prior to the strike, Kupersmith pointed out that the company had left the pilots no other choice but to strike. Ironically, Kupersmith had represented Lorenzo during Continental's bankruptcy, yet he came to be trusted by the unions and exercised a great deal of influence over their decision making. This influence lasted throughout the duration of the strike, although many pilots today question his abrupt turnabout in November 1989 when he recommended they call off the strike.

Management's Responses

Eastern's corporate communicators, many of whom were sensitive to the realities of the pilots' unrest, were being ignored by the decision makers. In an anonymous survey of public relations professionals on the subject of ethical challenges, taken by the author in mid-1988, a respondent who identified himself only as a "member of corporate communications with Eastern Airlines" complained: "Our management has its own agenda and it doesn't seem to have anything to do with what is good for our employees. This puts me in a real ethical dilemma. Do I quit and 'take a stand for what is right?' or stay and try to see if I can change things?"[36]

This claim is supported when one views the sluggishness in which corporate spokesmen responded to pilot agitation tactics beginning in 1988. Pilot activity took off with vigor in the first quarter of the year, yet company responses were few and often were in the form of refusal to comment.

By the end of the year, Eastern's management and pilots had met each other coming and going at the courthouse door. A number of suits and countersuits between the company and its unions had exhausted all parties concerned. Government officials and newspaper editorials were pleading for a truce. Frank Lorenzo and Eastern's management were exhausted from "putting out fires" set by labor discord. *Miami Herald* business writer David Lyons noted:

"Read my lips," said Eastern Airlines President Philip Bakes. "The company is not for sale." That Bakes even has to make such a statement is a symbol of the Miami-based carrier's frustrated labor policies. Eastern has proven to be a much more complex situation to resolve than its new owners had ever dreamed.[37]

Still maintaining avoidance methods, they brought their concerns to the public, a new tactic for the previously aloof management. Bakes submitted to interviews and met with business leaders and travel professionals. He blamed their cash shortage on business travelers who had fled the airline amid public concerns about airline safety. Lorenzo, too, began granting interviews—a rarity for him. Lorenzo argued publicly that if Eastern could get big concessions from labor it would survive.

Management responded to the safety probe with a full-page newspaper ad in which the company "welcomed" the investigation. *The Falcon* addressed the safety issue, at long last, on the front page of its May/June 1988 issue. With the headline, "Eastern Has Its Problems, But SAFETY Isn't One of Them," the publication set about to counter some of the accusations the pilots had made. A cartoon on the editorial page pointed to the "real" safety violations in its depictions of a giant pilot, mechanic, and flight attendant standing on a crumpling airplane. The caption read, "Safety Violation: *Loose Nuts on Aircraft*." [38] Frank Lorenzo's letter to *The Miami Herald* regarding "Texas/Eastern bashing" was reprinted in that issue as well. In that letter, Lorenzo defended management's decisions in the past:

> Texas Air is committed to Eastern's future. We understand the reluctance to change. What we do not understand is the unwillingness to recognize that Eastern must change in order to have a future.[39]

Interestingly, the front page of the last *Falcon* published before the strike (February 1989) took no notice of impending crisis and serves as another indicator that management did not feel the strike was going to be of the magnitude it turned out to be. *Falcon* headlines read fairly innocuously: "Once Again, Eastern Clocks in First," "Paint-n-Polish Promotes EAL pride," "EAL Employees Give Kids the World," and "Eastern Offers Super Coupons to Customers."

As the IAM's thirty-day cooling-off period came closer

to an end, Eastern's vice president of human resources Tom Matthews sent a memorandum to the pilots in which he argued against Kupersmith's advice to strike with the following six points:

1. The IAM needs EASTERN's pilots in order to shut the company down and risk us going out of business.

2. The IAM's pay demands for an increase are unreasonable. EASTERN's pilots may be asked to shut EASTERN down to support the IAM's demand for an additional 8%. It just doesn't make sense to help them increase the inequity from an existing 28% to 36%.

3. Although Kupersmith feels that in the event of bankruptcy, "stockholders, creditors, and employees will take a haircut," some disagree. Other widely respected financial analysts have indicated that if a bankruptcy occurs, the stockholders and creditors will probably come out just fine. The only sure thing is that the employees lose.

4. On Tuesday, February 14, the MEC completely overhauled its contract negotiating committee. The Chairman was replaced and new members were added, thus increasing the committee from three to five members. This has already created delay.

5. "Super mediation" with the IAM has been ordered by the NMB to begin on February 22nd and
continue through midnight, March 3, at an out-of-
town location. This will likely require the pilot
negotiations to be tabled until sometime in mid-
March.

6. The reality of this situation is that it is unlikely
that final agreement on both a fence [agreement]
and the economics of a new collective bargaining
agreement will be reached before March 3. Therefore, you will have to decide whether you want to
close down EASTERN before knowing whether an
agreement can be reached.[40]

In this and subsequent communications, Matthews
pleaded with the pilots not to let the IAM push them into
a hasty decision and questioned the arbitrary nature of
the pilots' deadlines.

On February 21, 1989, IAM president and general
chairman Charles Bryan asked the pilots for their support
in a letter:

We need your help to save Eastern before it is completely dismantled by Lorenzo. We are asking for
your support in the final days of the countdown and
we are asking you to honor and join us in our picket
lines if we are forced to strike. Now, more than
ever before, we must stick together. . . . We have

always supported the Pilots and Flight Attendants in the past and you have our pledge of solidarity and full support if you are ever forced to strike in the future.[41]

On March 1, all pilots received a videotape from Frank Lorenzo in which he claimed a fair and equitable contract proposal was being presented to them. ALPA responded with "much work still needs to be done"[42] and refused the company's offer for a fence agreement.

CONCLUSIONS

The pilots entered 1988 firing from the hip. Their flag issue, safety, had caught the attention of high government officials. Actual membership was growing as they attracted support from pilots from other airlines, as well as the public at large. Their rhetorical methods were in full gear, not the least of which included solidification tactics designed to unite pilots and their families—a tactic which had been sorely missing from The Resistance.

However, their feverish zeal for the safety issue may have contributed to its undoing. The pilots commanded a great deal of media attention for their cause; but in light of Transportation Secretary Burnley's report confirming the safety of Eastern's planes, the public began to spurn the safety issue as nothing more than scare tactics and union antics.

In spite of this setback with their flag issue, the pilots and other union groups had succeeded in raising Frank Lorenzo to the status of one of the most hated men in

America. Once his management tactics had been made public, even his staunchest allies could find little to say in his defense. Wall Street was becoming increasingly nervous as a head-to-head confrontation between Eastern's management and labor came closer to reality. The single greatest question in the minds of all was whether the pilots would join the strike. Without the pilots, the IAM had little hope of winning. With them, however, the effects of such a job action could be disastrous.

By mid-year, the pilots had lost faith in management and were stoically "girding for war." The impending loss of the shuttle was a devastating blow because of its cultural significance, and very likely pushed any undecided pilots past the point of no return. With their financial advisors assuring them they could save the airline by forcing Lorenzo to sell, the pilots sided with the IAM.

The events of 1988 shook loose some of management's traditional aloofness. Although still maintaining avoidance techniques of counterpersuasion, company leaders became more visible as they appealed to the public to see their side of things. The results, at least in the view of the pilots, was that of "too little, too late." To the end, management did not believe the pilots would walk.

NOTES

1. Vice president of Flight Operations, letter to all check pilots, March 1, 1989.

2.   David Lyons, "EAL Pilots Threaten Walkout, Atlanta Deal Riles Union," *The Miami Herald*, February 12, 1988, A1.

3.   David Lyons, "EAL Acknowledges Deal with Orion," *The Miami Herald*, February 13, 1988, D5.

4.   Gregg Fields, "Judge: EAL Can't Hire Orion As Backup," *The Miami Herald*, February 13, 1988, D5.

5.   Geoffrey Tomb and Arnold Markowitz, "Pieces of Engine Fall From Plane, Start Fire," *The Miami Herald*, February 16, 1988, A1.

6.   Associated press, "Flight Crew Has No New Clues on Jetliner That Cracked Open," *The Miami Herald*, February 13, 1988, A1.

7.   "Eastern Pilots Blast FAA Report on Safety," *The Miami Herald*, June 9, 1988, D11.

8.   "Pilots' Information Channel Number 5," a communication from the Air Line Pilots Association, February 23, 1989.

9.   "Eastern Flying Blind," *The Miami Herald*, May 12, 1988, A26.

10.   David Lyons and Martin Merzer, "As Eastern Is Slowly Dismantled, So Are Lives, Employees Who

Survived Painful Cutbacks Live on the Edge," *The Miami Herald*, November 13, 1988, A1.

11.   David Lyons, "Pilots May Back Walkout," *The Miami Herald*, February 10, 1989, F16.

12.   "Pilots Get An Upbeat Message," *The Miami Herald*, January 19, 1988, B4.

13.   "Editorial," *Eastern Pilot's Checklist*, February-March 1988, 1.

14.   Lawrence H. Summers, "A Traveler's Lament," *Eastern Pilot's Checklist*, April 1988, 3.

15.   "Dear Eastern Pilots. . . ," *Eastern Pilot's Checklist*, April 1988, 4-5.

16.   Jack Bavis, Dan Vician, and Buzz Wright, "Support Your Eastern Pilot's Hostage Fund," *Eastern Pilot's Checklist*, April 1988, 15.

17.   Bavis, Master Chairman's Report.

18.   Undated letter sent to all Eastern pilots from Pilots With Another View.

19.   "Selected Letters Concerning Pilots With Another View," *Eastern Pilot's Checklist*, June 1988, 4.

20. "Captain Stephens Gives Up On ALPA. . . And Wright George Gives Up On Captain Stephens," *Eastern Pilot's Checklist*, June 1988, 16.

21. "And Still More Letters Concerning Pilots With Another View," *Eastern Pilot's Checklist*, September 1988, 15.

22. "Editorial," *Eastern Pilot's Checklist*, May 1988, 1.

23. For example, Paul F. Eschenfelder, Jr., "Houston Deserves More from Texas Air," reprinted from *The Houston Chronicle*, September 4, 1988; "Frank Lorenzo and the Future of Newark," an editorial reprinted from *Crain's New York Business*, September 1988; "The Amazing Mr. Lorenzo. . . ," an editorial reprinted from *The New Jersey Record*, August 25, 1988; and "Gratitude or Vitriol?" reprinted from *Aviation Business Magazine*, August 1988.

24. Michael Ennis, "Sky King," *Business Month Magazine*, September 1988.

25. "Can You Pass This Texas Air Management Aptitude Test?" *Eastern Pilot's Checklist*, September 1988, 10-11.

26. Kenneth J. Oden, "A Memo to Management from One of the Junkyard Dogs," *Eastern Pilot's Checklist*,

November-December 1988, 2.

27.   Captain Eddie Rickenbacker, "I Believe in Prayer," reprinted from *Guideposts Magazine*, 1945, in *Eastern Pilot's Checklist*, January 1989, 26-27.

28.   Jeffrey R. Hall, "Are Pilots Wimps?" *Eastern Pilot's Checklist*, February-March 1988, 8.

29.   Ronald Hoffmeyer, "Another of Our Wounded Pauses to Say Goodbye. . . ," *Eastern Pilot's Checklist*, February-March 1988, 9.

30.   *Eastern Pilot's Checklist*, August 1988, 11.

31.   Andy Gambardella, "Thirty Pieces of Silver," *Eastern Pilot's Checklist*, May 1988, 13.

32.   "Pilots' Forum," *Air Line Pilot*, April 1988, 56.

33.   "Pilots' Forum," *Air Line Pilot*, April 1988, 56.

34.   "Pilots' Forum," *Air Line Pilot*, May 1988, 2.

35.   "Pilots' Forum," *Air Line Pilot*, May 1988, 2.

36.   Results of this survey were later published in *The Florida Speech Communicator's Journal*, Fall 1989.

37.   David Lyons, "For Managers, Cuts are Key to

Survival," *The Miami Herald*, December 4, 1988, F1.

38. Cartoon featured in *The Falcon*, May/June 1988, 3.

39. Reprinted from *The Miami Herald*, April 11, 1988, "Readers' Forum."

40. Tom Matthews and Frank Causey to all Eastern pilots, February 14, 1989.

41. Charles Bryan to Eastern pilots, February 21, 1989.

42. Western Union Mailgram to individual pilots, March 4, 1989, 4.

5

WAR!

We were united;
we were professional;
we were right.
—ALPA letter to pilots calling off strike[1]

The strike at Eastern Airlines reflected a classic labor
struggle. It tested the ability of big labor to re-establish
itself, but risked a major setback should Lorenzo, a noted
union adversary, prevail. In addition, the strike provided
an early examination for newly elected President George
Bush. Already, the pilots were disappointed at Bush's
refusal of the NMB's request to name an emergency
board to delay the March 4 strike. Later that same year,
Bush vetoed House of Representatives legislation calling
for a Congressional panel of inquiry, thus effectively

ending the walkout. The move so infuriated the pilots that the saying emerged, "When George Bush looks out upon his 'thousand points of light,' he's really seeing the bonfires formed as the pilots of Eastern Airlines burn their Republican party membership cards."

Faced with a panicky traveling public, the company pulled its consumer advertising and began working on a new marketing campaign geared largely toward retaining its frequent fliers' loyalty during the strike. Meanwhile, the carrier grounded more planes, and a federal judge in Miami struck a blow against the company when he refused to block the pilots from striking in support of the machinists. In a lawsuit, Eastern argued that the walkout could bankrupt the carrier. Meanwhile, an additional 2,500 nonstriking workers were laid off.

The strike proved to be a boon for Eastern's competitors—as they reported major traffic increases and cut back on discount tickets to charge higher fares. Eastern agreed to sell two routes and other operations to USAir for $85 million, in an effort to fund its battle with the striking workers. At the same time, the IAM was lobbying TWA chairman Carl Icahn to renew talks to acquire the company.

Worried about reports of a possible bankruptcy filing, ticket holders scrambled for refunds, only to be caught in the red tape when the company filed its Chapter 11 petition. Lorenzo's bankruptcy strategy had worked well for him at Continental, where he had successfully negotiated with the bankruptcy court to have union contracts negated. This time, however, the pilots had learned their lesson and had no intention of letting that happen again. Bankruptcy law, which had been changed by Congress since the Continental strike, specified that a company can't abrogate a labor contract without first negotiating with the union. Likewise, the union must negotiate with the company. Therefore, the pilots renewed negotiations with the company, depriving Lorenzo of any grounds for convincing the court to end their contract.

Judge Burton Lifland, a veteran of many big bankruptcy cases was named to hear the company's petition. Lorenzo had filed for bankruptcy in the Southern District of New York instead of Eastern's hometown, Miami. The reason for this may have been that New York's bankruptcy courts were believed to be more sympathetic to management than Miami's bankruptcy courts. In addition, Eastern's bankruptcy attorney Harvey Miller practiced in New York and had enjoyed a long-standing relationship with Judge Lifland.

Of all the personalities involved in the strike, the most visible were Charlie Bryan, the rabble rousing head of the machinists' union, and Frank Lorenzo, the icy head of TAC. With missionary zeal, Bryan was throwing everything he had into the fight to find a savior for the airline before it was completely cannibalized; Lorenzo, with low-key stubbornness, was insistent that the company was still a viable operation and he, alone, could save it. As the strike wore on, however, the two antagonists remained curiously out of sight. Abraham Gitlow, professor emeritus of economics at New York University, was quoted in *The Miami Herald* as saying Lorenzo had backed away because "everytime he comes to the forefront, he gets people aggravated." Although Lorenzo had made some appearances, his apparent effort to improve his image failed. After Barbara Walters, on March 17, asked him how it felt to be the most hated man in America, he withdrew from public view. As for Bryan, Gitlow said, "He won a number of victories earlier on, but he's not having victories now—the situation is grinding its way towards what will be for everyone a very unhappy outcome."[2]

By March 13, Eastern had managed to get only 104 flights back into the air, far short of even its scaled-back goal of 126 flights a day. The company unveiled options for fliers holding tickets. Meanwhile, ALPA asked the bankruptcy court to appoint a trustee to administer the airline's affairs.

With all the impact of a broken home, the strike bared long-festering anger among its employees. The pilots, still angry with the machinists for refusing concessions that may have prevented the sale of the airline in the first place, were uneasy with the alliance. Nonunion employees may have suffered most, psychologically, as they had no benefit of picket lines, huzzahs, or union-sponsored support efforts. The company began advertising for pilots to replace the thousands who refused to cross machinists' picket lines.

Judge Lifland ordered the appointment of an examiner with broad powers to oversee creditors' rights during Eastern's reorganization under Chapter 11. David Shapiro, a Washington lawyer, was appointed as examiner. Shapiro had served formerly as the court-appointed special master who brought about a settlement in the Agent Orange lawsuit. Judge Lifland gave Shapiro broad powers to investigate all past transactions between Eastern and Texas Air or Continental, to consider viable plans for the reorganization of Eastern, to meet with creditors and employees to discuss their concerns, and to act as a facilitator and mediator among the parties.

A number of potential buyers emerged. Former baseball commissioner Peter Ueberroth's $464 million offer was rejected after Texas Air said the offer had been topped by an unidentified bidder. Pilot leaders met with financier Jay Pritzker about his interest in buying the carrier, as Donald Trump worked out final details toward his purchase of the shuttle. Spirits rose when Eastern agreed to be acquired by the Ueberroth group. The three unions agreed to a five-year contract sought by Ueberroth, but the deal fell through after Frank Lorenzo refused to cede his control of the company to a bankruptcy court trustee for a transitional period. Immediately afterward, union representatives asked TWA head Carl Icahn to make a bid for the firm.

Despite these disappointments, the coalition between pilots and machinists continued to hold, a point not completely pleasing to business observers. *The Wall Street Journal* accused the groups of "Ahab Unionism," and compared them to Captain Ahab of Melville's *Moby Dick*, in their singleminded vendetta against Frank Lorenzo.[3] Indeed, the strikers did hate Frank Lorenzo, but they fervently loved Eastern Airlines, a point often noted by members of the media. Columnist William F. Buckley observed that the unions would go to great lengths to revive their airline, and noted "EAL's average employee has been with that airline an incredible 18 years, a measure of the special allure of a special company about which people feel as ardently as people do about the Boston Red Sox." Buckley went on to comment on the unions' singleminded hatred for Frank Lorenzo and bemoaned, "Charles Bryan, the head of the Machinists. . . would, one gathers, rather prefer a nuclear war to feeding one more Eastern erg of manpower into Frank Lorenzo's maw." The only remedy for the company's woes, as suggested by Buckley, lay in a successful buyout.[4]

In April, Texas Air pulled Eastern off the auction block and announced a plan to shed certain assets and return the carrier to service. Several bidders, including Chicago Research & Trading Group chairman, Joseph Ritchie, remained interested in the firm. Judge Lifland approved the sale of the shuttle to Donald Trump on May 17 and scheduled a hearing for two competing bids; however, court-appointed examiner David Shapiro said he was dissatisfied with both bids—one from a group led by William Howard, former chairman of Piedmont Aviation, and the other from Ritchie. Creditors began pressuring the court for guarantees that some of the proceeds of the sale of assets would go to them.

The "New Eastern" was launched in June, as the carrier announced plans to resume service on its new, smaller route system, and began slashing fares to entice passengers back. Meanwhile, the company trimmed the pay of top management an additional 10 percent, in an effort to placate creditors after the striking unions offered to take pay cuts in support of Ritchie's bid for the airline. The company presented a deal to the pilots with new, scaled-back contract offers that added pay cuts on top of previously sought benefit cuts and would have brought only about 25 percent of them back to work. The pilots rejected the proposal, and in reference to the "New Eastern," began calling themselves, the "Real Eastern."

The New Eastern did not fare well with the traveling public. A consumer group warned travelers that Eastern's comeback was risky. Public Citizen and the Aviation Consumer Action Project (ACAP), both affiliated with consumer activist Ralph Nader, "questioned the qualifications of new pilots hired by the Miami-based carrier." In a memo, the groups showed the airline had lowered standards for pilots and copilots, many of whom were still being trained.[5] U.S. Senator Thomas Eagleton gave the following commentary on St. Louis television:

For United Flight 232 it was a miracle and a man. The *miracle*—184 people survived the crash of the jet as it flip-flopped into a fireball in Sioux City, Iowa last Wednesday. The *man* was pilot A.C. Haynes, a 33-year veteran with United—Haynes guided a plane that couldn't be guided. He brought in a plane that couldn't be brought in. . . . If the plane had been Eastern Flight 232, there might *not*

have been *any* survivors. Eastern owner Frank
Lorenzo is cranking out brand new pilots as quickly
as possible to get his planes in the air. If the
Eastern strike is ever settled, he wants to keep the
lower paid, inexperienced pilots and let experienced
pilots go elsewhere. . . . People on United Flight
232 can thank God Pilot A.C. Haynes hadn't been
replaced by someone just out of flight training.[6]

The strike moved to a stalemate as Judge Lifland
granted the company numerous extensions to file its
reorganization plans—indicating some confidence in its
ability to restart at two-thirds its former size. In August,
discouraged and scared, a number of the pilots returned
to work. Although the union still maintained the backing
to pursue the strike, resolve within the ranks was weak-
ening. In September, the pilots dumped Jack Bavis, who
was urging them to abandon their picket line and replaced him with a more militant leader, Skip Copeland.
Copeland, "a proven gladiator" who was challenged with
breathing new life into the strike, urged his compatriots
to "hang tough and see this struggle through. . . one
more day than Frank Lorenzo."[7] ALPA national members voted to continue paying strike benefits to the
Eastern pilots, buying time for the embattled union, yet
it became apparent that the pilots from other airlines
were growing tired of financing (through assessments) a
losing fight.

Meanwhile, Eastern's creditors, unhappy with the
vagueness of the "new" Eastern's plans for emerging

from bankruptcy, asked experts from Ernst & Young and Goldman, Sachs & Co. to devise alternate approaches to a reorganization. Lorenzo, on the other hand, insisted Eastern was exceeding its goals for getting back into operation.

In November, the U.S. House of Representatives sent President Bush legislation for a panel of inquiry to investigate the strike. Bush, who earlier that year had praised Solidarity union leader Lech Walesa and Polish union members at the AFL-CIO convention, vetoed H.R. 1231, effectively dashing the pilots' best hope for a satisfactory settlement. ALPA president Henry Duffy responded: "George Bush promised us a thousand points of light to illuminate a kinder, gentler America, but so far he's given us only one—and that's a bonfire on the White House grounds, where they're burning every bill that supports the worker." IAM president George Kourpias put it more strongly: "By failing to sign the Eastern bill, the President embraced the meanest worker-hating boss in the nation, Frank Lorenzo."[8]

Although there was hope that Congress could override the veto when it returned in January, Eastern's MEC voted unanimously on November 24 to end the 264-day strike and return unconditionally to work. The MEC commented: "No one can say we didn't give our best shot at making this strike work. We were united; we were professional; we were right. But the cards have been stacked against us throughout this battle in the courts and by President Bush."[9] The "most emotional strike in U.S. airline history"[10] had been broken. Some observers at the time believed a merger between the streamlined Eastern and Continental was a certainty after the company emerged from Chapter 11, anticipated in early 1990.[11]

COMMUNICATION STRATEGIES OF PILOTS AND MANAGEMENT

Pilot Responses

With the walkout, the pilots' agitation activities reached a critical mass. They were, in their own words, "at war" with the company. Their communication strategies continued to include petitioning of the establishment and promulgation through exploitation of the mass media, but the biggest communication challenge to pilot leaders was keeping solidarity within the ranks.

Because the pilots were no longer receiving mail at their airport domiciles, union correspondence had to be adjusted. Most of the communications came in the form of letters and tapes mailed to the pilots' homes. Just prior to the walkout, members of the newly formed Strike/Operations Committee (STOP) urged the pilots to place their trust in the negotiating committee and the MEC and were reminded that if the company tried to negotiate with them directly, they were to "show them the door and remind them to whom they need to talk." At the bottom of the page of this and every STOP letter was printed the slogan, "Let's Go Together—Just Say No!"[12]

Eastern's MEC concluded that it was in the best interest of the pilots to honor the IAM picket line and balloted the membership. "The reasons for this position," leaders argued, "are based on the logical conclusion that this is in the best interest of the PILOTS, not the IAM and not Charlie Bryan." MEC communications explained to the pilots that Lorenzo's empire was close to broke, but that if he could get cash from the sale of the Air Shuttle or the transfer of other assets, like the Latin America routes, he would be in "a far better position to inflict serious, probably fatal, damage on us." [13] (Lorenzo did, in fact, manage to sell the Latin America routes later that year).

Subsequent letters to the pilots outlined their rights and protections during the strike, insurance benefits available to them, and opportunities for short-term loans. Once the strike began, strongly worded letters urged the pilots to fight harder. They were told to expect dirty tricks, such as being listed by management as having crossed the picket line when that was not the case. Unions leaders told pilots they had a sworn affidavit from an Eastern flight attendant who stated she was offered money if she would put on a pilot's uniform and cross the picket line to demoralize pilots who were not crossing. Another story was told of a pilot's wife who was in the hospital and was called by management and threatened with loss of insurance coverage. Still another relayed the tale of someone who was not a striking pilot who appeared at the picket line in a pilot's uniform and engaged in behavior which would discredit Eastern pilots. The pilots were cautioned to check out rumors with the local communications centers before falling for "dirty tricks." Additionally, they were warned that anyone not maintaining a professional approach on the picket line should be removed immediately.[14]

The pilots were gearing up for the long haul. When asked how long the sympathy strike would last, one pilot suggested they put the answer this way: "One day longer than Frank Lorenzo."[15] The response caught on as the rallying cry for the duration of the strike. Communications urged them to "stay on an even keel and not get too high or too low when we see or hear media reports." Strike sympathizers were advised to tape all telephone calls from management and instituted the "CAT" program, which included asking for company identification number, ALPA identification number, telling the caller the call was going to be taped, taping the call, then hanging up.[16]

ALPA national, representing pilots at forty-seven other airlines, approved strike benefits, interest-free loans, and other support for Eastern pilots participating in the sympathy strike. Throughout the strike, union leadership was careful to explain the individual pilot's rights under bankruptcy and other conditions as they developed. ALPA president Henry Duffy announced that the executive board authorized the following:

1. strike benefits of $2,400 monthly for each Eastern pilot engaging in the sympathy strike; and
2. interest-free loans of $2,000 for captains, $1,500

for first officers, and $1,200 for second officers to replace March 15 paychecks that Eastern management refused to issue for work already done.

In addition, union leaders agreed to seek agreements with other carriers providing that Eastern pilots would become employees of any carrier acquiring any part of Eastern's operation, with preservation of seniority.[17]

Strike leaders maintained an ongoing effort to keep the pilots from crossing the picket lines. One mailgram to the pilots urged them to "reach out to those few who have crossed the line." The letter referred to a group of pilots from United Airlines who had not observed that union's strike and had, as a result, suffered feelings of conflict and isolation that had never gone away. The letter urged, "We need to avoid that kind of human suffering at Eastern."[18]

Petitioning efforts included a mail blitz to Congress in support of the Senate version of H.R. 1231, which would require the creation of a presidential emergency board to investigate the dispute. Henry Duffy testified before the Senate judiciary committee in support of S. 544, a bill that would allow Eastern's creditors access to the assets of Texas Air, Continental, and Jet Capital.[19] Duffy questioned why George Bush was the first president ever to refuse a request from the NMB to appoint a presidential emergency board to investigate a labor-management dispute. Citing a *Boston Globe* article detailing the "revolving door" through which officials of Texas Air and the Reagan and Bush administrations have passed "as

they've gone from work for Lorenzo to work regulating
Lorenzo, or vice versa," Duffy soundly attacked the
integrity of the administration when he said in a teleconference,

"I'm not going to suggest that this lack of responsible action (by Bush) . . . has anything to do with
the fact that Frank Lorenzo is a $100,000 donor to
the Republican party . . . or with the fact that the
Bush aide who signed the letter informing Congress
of the President's decision not to appoint any
emergency board is a fresh recruit from TAC's
corporate offices." [20]

The pilots put further pressure on the Bush administration in April when they sponsored a full-page ad in *USA Today* detailing personnel relationships between Texas Air and the White House.

Another communication strategy, the Family Awareness program, was set up to keep the families united throughout the ordeal. Newsletters and assorted motivational material provided additional support. Information on stress management techniques, such as dealing with anger or beating insomnia, was provided for pilot families. Letters went out to school teachers asking for help in understanding should the pilots' children develop problems as a result of the strike.

The pilots were never out of touch with strike organizers. Daily communications kept the resistance efforts well oiled. They seized every opportunity to prevail, including pushing Florida's governor Bob Martinez to aid in the purchase of the airline through the investment of pension fund money. After giving the proposal some consideration, Martinez declined because of the volatile nature of the matter and concluded that the state should not invest pension fund money at that time.

Pilots leaders enhanced promulgation efforts by starting a program to contact future aviation professionals at job fairs, colleges, and other locations to make sure they understood why going to work at Eastern at the time would not be a good career decision. The program used the message, "We are holding the line for our future at Eastern Airlines and for your future as aviation professionals."[21] Additional efforts to gain public support were directed to travel professionals who were urged not to book on Eastern or Continental because "1. Lorenzo's airlines lead the nation in customer complaints, 2. Continental and Eastern are a bad risk for travel agents and passengers, 3. Lorenzo is incapable of improving his airlines, and 4. Booking away from Lorenzo is good for your community relations."[22]

Generally, the strike effort maintained momentum throughout the summer. One characteristically emotional message from the pilots appeared in the form of an ad in newspapers throughout the country. The ad featured a photograph of some striking Eastern pilots who had once been prisoners of war. Under the caption, "We Fought for the American Dream . . . We Are Now Fighting Against the American Nightmare—Frank Lorenzo," the ad included the following copy:

Frank Lorenzo recently said that the striking Eastern pilots have been "brainwashed." These men, who, unlike Lorenzo, have seen war and brainwashing first hand, know exactly what they are doing. They are fighting another war—a war against greed and power . . . . Please help protect our American Dream and don't fly Eastern until the strike has ended.[23]

Colleagues from other airlines offered moral support. An electronic bulletin board network available to the pilots shared the following anecdotes from a Piedmont pilot addressed to the "Eastern guys":

In BOS:[Boston, relaying a ground to air transmission between Boston tower and a TWA incoming flight]
Grd: TWA***pick up that Eastern DC-9 and follow him to . . . .
TWA: (Very deep voice) I THOUGHT EASTERN WAS ON STRIKE?!! (At this point [ground] was buried under numerous yuks, cackles, and other expressions of disgust at the scab s**theads.)
Grd: Gentlemen, gentlemen, I have traffic to control!!
TWA: They ain't gentlemen, they're SCABS![24]

In ORF: [Norfolk]
The Piedmont Captain was in his seat at the gate getting ready to go, when out of EA ops [opera-

tions] walked the King of Krap hisself [sic], escort-
ed by the station mgr. and a bodyguard. The PAI
Capt. was amazed when L_____ [Lorenzo]
looked up, pointed, and nudged his two bullet-stops,
er, companions: The Captain turned around to see
what s**thead was pointing and getting exercised
about and found his FE [flight engineer] mooning
F[rank] and the FO [first officer] give d—kless the
one-fingered salute. As the trio were then passing
in front of the airplane, he sounded the nosewell
horn so F[rank] could get a load of the FE giving
him the pressed-ham treatment. Us rednecks are so
easily entertained.[25]

The message concluded with an allusion to the strike's
rallying cry, "Hang in there guys. Jus' one humorous
day longer!"[26]

Frank Lorenzo remained at the center of polarization
efforts. An Associated Press report concluded that this
tactic "of focusing attention on Frank Lorenzo . . . as the
bad guy in the strike is beneficial for the employees" as
they were able to vent their feeling on the picket lines.
As the strike persisted, he was compared to Darth Vader
(evil villain from the movie *Star Wars*), and information
on management activities was called "news from the dark
side," in yet another allusion to the popular movie. At
other times, he was compared to the fictional character,
Peter Pan—as one pilot concluded that Lorenzo's restruc-
turing plan was being made real (à la Pan and Tinkerbell)
by clapping hands to signify belief. The *Kansas City*

Star ran an editorial cartoon that featured a Lorenzo character lying on a psychiatrist's couch with the doctor responding, "Don't worry, Mr. Lorenzo, you're not being paranoid—everyone *does* hate you."

In spite of their united hatred of Lorenzo, the pilots' faith in the strike started to slip in August. As Lorenzo continued to ride out the storm, a number of pilots crossed over and returned to work. The majority remained on strike, and union leadership continued to rally the troops. A rally in Washington concluded a 3,000 mile "march for justice" and attracted a number of congressmen, including Massachusetts Senator Ted Kennedy who said: "You are asking every member of the Congress to stand up for fairness and justice and equity—to stand up to Frank Lorenzo—and you deserve no less."[27]

Even after the strike ended, the pilots maintained the emotional metaphors of war saying, for example, "This is the kind of war that leaves no winners . . ." and "We have had much struggle, many obstacles and a lot of stormy waters in the battle."[28] They had fought a good fight, they argued, and they agreed with Marion Friday, a pilot's wife, who concluded:

In the history of the business journals, I hope that someday it will be noted that these individuals had the courage and stamina to stand up to men with no more than a passion for greed and few if any principles. The people of Eastern Air Lines tried to change the laws to govern unethical buyouts and takeovers. I hope that the history journals will also someday note that this fight was a success.[29]

Management's Responses

On the day after the walkout, Eastern headquarters was a ghost town. To the last minute, management had not believed the pilots would support the IAM's strike. The nonstriking employees were in shock. Communications were erratic and confusion prevailed until Lorenzo's plan for the new Eastern revitalized the demoralized employees.

Management responded immediately to the strike using the counterpersuasion method of rebuttal in the form of persistent letters and phone calls to the pilots. The pilots received an early response in the form of an open letter from Eastern to Farrell Kupersmith, the financial advisor who had encouraged to pilots to join in the strike. In that letter, the company argued with some of the primary points in Kupersmith's videotape regarding job protection, job security, and job guarantees. The letter was signed, "Names Withheld Because of ALPA fear and intimidation."[30] Subsequent letters were filled with grim projections of what would happen to their jobs if they didn't return immediately. The pilots were repeatedly told "that each day an Eastern aircraft doesn't fly, the chances decrease that it will ever fly again in Eastern colors with Eastern pilots in the cockpit."[31] Many of the strongly worded letters attempted to discredit the motivations of ALPA organizers, in an attempt to get the pilots back. One particularly inflammatory message

claimed that the thirty-four new hires Eastern had
acquired were superior in skill to those pilots they were
replacing. "The fact is," the letter continued, "one third
of the current MEC membership wouldn't measure up to
the qualification and experience standards needed to
make this class." [32] Comments such as "Eastern will not
surrender! Eastern will survive!" complemented the war
jargon of the pilots. In an interview conducted by
corporate communications staff member, Karen Ceremsak, company president Phil Bakes acknowledged that the
pilot walkout had resulted in the virtual shutdown of
Eastern. Bakes said what he had not foreseen was that
"Eastern pilots would be willing to join forces with
Charlie Bryan to drive the company into bankruptcy in
order to serve the Duffy-ALPA agenda."[33]

With the announcement of the new Eastern, the
company was engaging, at least in part, in the adjustment
technique of changing the name of the agency. In this
manner, the company was able to acknowledge past mis-
takes, while providing for itself a clean slate among the
traveling public. The trimmed down version of Eastern
was presented to the pilots via Western Union Mailgram.
Therein, the company explained that there were only
1,000-1,100 pilot jobs left to fill and encouraged them to
apply for those jobs before it was too late. In summa-
rizing this latest move, the letter stated, "We simply have
decided we had rather see Eastern survive—than see it
sold piecemeal and liquidated. We hope some of you
can understand our decision."[34]

The new Eastern was advertised to the public as a

"Brand New Eastern Airlines, With a Bunch of Old Pros." Advertising copy emphasized the experience of the people working for Eastern, especially the pilots. Cheap fares and the substantive advertising campaigns brought a positive response to the company, bought time for Frank Lorenzo, and provided a setback that the pilots were not able to survive.

CONCLUSIONS

Propelled by their hatred of Frank Lorenzo and convinced they could force the sale of the airline to a more acceptable owner, Eastern's pilots joined with the other unions in a strike that brought the airline to its knees in bankruptcy court. The pilots plunged immediately into petitioning strategy and engaged in talks between prospective buyers and the other unions. Solidification activities increased, and union organizers worked feverishly to hold the pilots together in the face of strong persuasive tactics by management. The family awareness project kept spouses and families included in their activities, and many spouses of pilots joined in the strike effort.

The pilots' war cry, "One day longer than Frank Lorenzo," may have proved to be part of their undoing. The Ueberroth deal fell through, in part, because the unions—their hatred prevailing—refused to accept even a brief period of continued work under the hated Lorenzo, even for a transitional period. There were other factors in the failure of the Ueberroth deal, but the reluctance on the part of the pilots to have any dealings with Lorenzo, certainly discouraged further efforts to work it out. As a result of the impasse, Lorenzo moved to his backup plan, that of a downsized Eastern, and bought himself enough time with the bankruptcy court to ride out the strike. With influential government officials sympathetic with Eastern's "legitimate" claim to power, the strike at this point was doomed.

NOTES

1. Air Line Pilots Association to all Eastern pilots and families via Western Union Mailgram, November 22, 1989.

2. Ted Reed, "Chief Eastern Protagonists Take a Back Seat," *The Miami Herald*, June 18, 1989, F1.

3. "Ahab Unionism," *The Wall Street Journal*, April 14, 1989, A14.

4. William F. Buckley, "Eastern Still Exudes Special Allure," *Pensacola News Journal*, June 20, 1989, A7.

5. David Field, "Nader Affiliates Warn Eastern Return Risky," *The Washington Times*, July 28, 1989, A12.

6. Senate Thomas Eagleton, "Commentary," KSDK Channel 5, St. Louis, Missouri, July 23, 1989.

7. Air Line Pilots Association to all Eastern pilots and families via Western Union Mailgram, September 8, 1989.

8. Air Line Pilots Association to all Eastern pilots and families via Western Union Mailgram, November 22, 1989.

9. EAL MEC Strike/Operations Committee to Eastern pilots, February 24, 1989.

10. Marcy Gordon, "Eastern's Not Out of Woods Yet," *Pensacola News Journal*, December 24, 1989, D1.

11. Gordon.

12. Eal MEC Strike/Operations Committee to Eastern pilots, February 24, 1989.

13. Bob Breslin, chairman, Local Executive Council #18, to all pilots, February 16, 1989.

14. Air Line Pilots Association to all Eastern pilots and families via Western Union Mailgram, March 13, 1989.

15. Air Line Pilots Association to all Eastern pilots and families via Western Union Mailgram, March 17, 1989.

16. ALPA letter, March 17, 1989.

17. Air Line Pilots Association to all Eastern pilots and families, via Western Union Mailgram, March 14, 1989.

18. Air Line Pilots Association to all Eastern pilots and families via Western Union Mailgram, March 16, 1989.

19. Air Line Pilots Association to all Eastern pilots and families via Western Union Mailgram, March 17, 1989.

20. Teleconference sponsored by Eastern Pilots' Strike Operations Committee and directed to all pilots and their families, March 22, 1989.

21. Teleconference, March 22, 1989.

22. Letter signed "The Employees of Eastern," to travel professionals, June 7, 1989.

23. This advertisement, sponsored by ALPA, ran in major newspapers across the country, including *USA Today*, May 26, 1989.

24. Compuserve Bulletin Board, September 20, 1989.

25. Compuserve.

26. Compuserve.

27. ALPA Mailgram, September 8, 1989.

28. Report featuring an interview with company president Phil Bakes sent to all Eastern employees, November 22, 1989.

29. ALPA mailgram, November 22, 1989.

30. Eastern Airlines to Farrell Kupersmith sent to all Eastern pilots via Western Union Mailgram, March 21, 1989.

31. Eastern Airlines to individual pilots via Western Union Mailgram, March 21, 1989.

32. Eastern Airlines letter to Farrell Kupersmith, March 21, 1989.

33. Interview with Eastern president Phil Bakes conducted by Karen Ceremsak and sent to all employees March 15, 1989.

34. Eastern Airlines to individual pilots via Western Union Mailgram, May 4, 1989.

6

THE MORNING AFTER

No one seemed to give a damn.
—Pat Broderick, twenty-two year veteran pilot[1]

The pilots agreed to go back to work, but there were no jobs when they returned. In fact, none of the sympathy-striking pilots were allowed back on company property, at first. Eastern had been radically pared down since they had gone out on strike, and the company had only about half the pilots it had had previously. Of these, approximately 1,000 were newly hired pilots. The unions sued Eastern for the 1,000 jobs it had lost to nonunion workers.

Lorenzo's position with Eastern's creditors weakened substantially, as he retreated from pledges to repay debts in full and in cash. A subsequent promise to pay them at a rate of about fifty cents per dollar due them was withdrawn as well. A committee of unsecured creditors rejected an offer of repayment of about twenty-five cents on the dollar and voted to seek a bankruptcy court trustee to run the airline. In April 1990, after backing away from it several times previously, Judge Burton R. Lifland took control of Eastern Airlines away from parent TAC and its chairman, Frank Lorenzo. Former Continental Airlines president Martin R. Shugrue was appointed as trustee. Shugrue's effort to turn Eastern around never got off the ground, and in January 1991, Eastern Airlines, once one of the nation's largest airlines, announced that it had stopped flying the night before and would begin to sell off its planes and other assets.

In the meantime, the pilots won a few victories, albeit hollow. First, a federal appeals court ruled that the company should have reinstated striking pilots who returned to work before it put replacement pilots in its cockpits. In addition, the safety issue came to fruition when the company and nine employees were indicted in New York on charges of failing to perform mandatory maintenance on Eastern aircraft and falsifying related records. A former Eastern foreman pleaded guilty to charges that he had ignored vital maintenance and safety repairs and then falsified records to make it appear the work had been done. The company and the other eight top managers pleaded not guilty but later changed their pleas to guilty.

Judge Lifland had appointed Washington lawyer David I. Shapiro as examiner of Eastern and granted him broad powers to resolve Eastern's bankruptcy quickly. Shapiro's subsequent report showed that TAC underpaid Eastern by as much as $403 million for assets acquired in a dozen transactions since 1987.

Once the dust had settled, the country looked in horror at the carnage. Nearly 45,000 people had been put out of work over the past three years, and an airline many thought of as a national fixture was gone. TWA chairman Carl Icahn, who once had been a suitor for the airline, was quoted as saying, "Frank [Lorenzo] was like Captain Ahab. He was obsessed with beating Charlie Bryan and the unions."[2] Conservative, pro-business outsiders noted that Lorenzo had not had the persuasive ability or the credibility to make it at Eastern. John Backe, the former CBS president said, "Lorenzo killed an airline. If he did it just to kill a union, that's unthinkable. And I think he did. It's hard for me to fathom."[3]

Business Week reporter Aaron Bernstein pondered the question of whether Eastern's fate would have been any different if Lorenzo had taken a softer approach. He wrote, "It's possible that even the most cooperative of managers might not have been able to bring Eastern's divided unions together. Still, the company's employees had shown a willingness to do almost anything to keep their jobs and their company going, provided they were included in the process. Lorenzo never saw that."[4]

COMMUNICATION STRATEGIES OF PILOTS AND MANAGEMENT

Pilot Responses

The pilots suffered when the strike ended. Although ALPA national elected to maintain limited strike benefits, many were forced to move from their homes. Some lost everything to foreclosure or bankruptcy, but few showed any regrets. In their minds, they had paid the price for the industry. Lorenzo's Eastern and Continental were no longer viable operations, but the pilots' punishment for their effort was severe. Twenty-two year veteran Pat Broderick reflected the apparent views of many in a *Newsweek* essay in which he said: "We [the pilots] chose to join our mechanics and flight attendants in a sympathy strike we hoped would force someone to look at the situation and realize that capitalism can run amok. That even free enterprise must act responsibly, and that government must maintain some degree of oversight to prevent self-destructive excesses within the system. . . . I do not regret having fought to save my company and improve the quality of its service. I do regret that no one seemed to give a damn."[5]

Bitterness remained after the disillusionment many of the pilots suffered toward national institutions. They felt as if they had been ignored by the Department of Transportation when they were presenting their case on the safety issue. Bankruptcy Judge Lifland had sided with Lorenzo on virtually every substantive issue, and at the end, President Bush had vetoed their only hope for resolving their problems.

Communication dwindled. Huckabee recalls that even rumors were practically nonexistent at Eastern after the strike. The few pilots who were recalled distrusted each other. ALPA pins were forbidden on the coat lapel.[6]

Resentment toward "the scabs" persists to date. Currently a list of the names of Eastern pilots or replacements who crossed the picket line is circulating among ALPA pilots across the nation. No one claims to have developed the list, but its existence virtually guarantees the names on the list will never work in the (unionized) airline business again.

Management Responses

Eastern's bosses had no need to communicate with the pilots after the strike ended, primarily because they had no use for the pilots. The "new" Eastern declined rapidly, while pilots of the "real" Eastern mourned. Little contact was made with the pilots, except in cases in which they [the pilots] were employee creditors. In those cases, they received information from the company only as mandated by the bankruptcy court.

CONCLUSIONS

There was little to comfort the pilots after the strike, except their own rhetoric. Comments such as "Even though Lorenzo won, he lost,"[7] brought little cheer to the unemployed pilots, whose tightly focused skills gave them few opportunities in the job market. They were defeated and had no place to go. Informal reports revolved around divorces, accidents, and suicides as a result of the situation. ALPA does not release names or information on members, so it is difficult to determine how many found other airline jobs, but the scuttlebutt in pilot circles is that the numbers are few. Many are working in menial capacities at jobs for which they are grossly overqualified, just to make ends meet. Their only communications are from ALPA, and those are dwindling in relevant information. Still, there is little evidence of regret. To the pilots, their fight was for "freedom, liberty, justice . . . and the realization they had a duty toward their predecessors and followers. When called, they answered; symbolically bloodied and battered, they endured."[8]

NOTES

1.   Pat Broderick, "A Fed-Up Pilot Speaks Out," *Newsweek*, April 23, 1990, 8.

2.   Aaron Bernstein, *Grounded: Frank Lorenzo and the Destruction of Eastern Airlines* (New York: Simon and Schuster, 1990), 230.

3.   Bernstein, 230.

4.   Bernstein, 236.

5.   Broderick, 8.

6. Captain Don Huckabee, "The Fall of Eastern, Lorenzo's Legacy," *Air Line Pilot* 60 (March 1991): 16-17.

7. Bernstein, 214.

8. Huckabee, 17.

OBSERVATIONS ON AN ORGANIZATIONAL CRISIS

Communication theory predicts that when an agitative group bearing the characteristics of the pilots of Eastern Airlines (i.e., high actual and potential membership, high level of rhetorical sophistication) goes up against an establishment with equally high critical variables (power, strength of ideology, and rhetorical sophistication), the establishment can always successfully avoid or suppress agitative movements.[1] The prediction was supported in this study of labor conflict at Eastern Airlines. The establishment at Eastern maintained, primarily, an avoidance posture throughout the agitation period and successfully withstood the onslaught. By "successfully withstanding," that is to say the pilots did not "win" in their attempt to unseat the management of Eastern. The result, as the history books will soon reflect, was that management and labor at the airline "successfully" pulled each other over a cliff.

That Frank Lorenzo and his management prevailed under these circumstances is due, primarily, to their advantage in "legitimate power," as discussed in the conclusion portion of Chapter 2. Government agencies, judicial observers, and even the media gave the benefit of the doubt to the company at every call. This is irrefutable and axiomatic of agitative conflict. The question remains, however, as to whether things might have been different had one side or the other chosen different conflict strategies. Since history cannot be relived, speculations are best based on an analysis of certain turning points during the crisis.

The first turning point occurred in 1987, shortly after Texas Air took control of the company. The pilots and other unions were wary, to be sure, but they *were* subdued. Analysts have noted that labor wasn't the biggest problem Eastern faced when Texas Air acquired the company in 1986, and the pilots and flight attendants had already made considerable cost-cutting adjustments.[2] Lorenzo's biggest mistake then, was in cutting the employees out of the process—through puppet management, through harsh, non-negotiable work rules, and through his obsessive hatred of unions. Frank Lorenzo, with his Harvard MBA, should have known better. Every first year business student knows that when employees feel they have no control over their lives, they will frequently band together (via unions) and seize control—often at the cost of organizational unity. Lorenzo's Eastern proved the truth to the saying, "Power doesn't corrupt—powerlessness does." *Any* conciliatory gesture from him might have turned the tragic tide of events.

The pilots were desperate for information on the company's plan for the future, but none was forthcoming.[3] Lorenzo made no attempt to assure the pilots that their jobs and the company were important to him. Instead, he brutalized them and began cannibalizing the company. In response, the pilots banded together, forming a phalanx in defense of their beloved Eastern and, in their minds, their honor.

A second critical point during the conflict occurred during the summer of 1989 after all realistic hopes of a buyout had collapsed. The new Eastern was to be about half the size of its former self. Under those conditions, there was no way all of the striking pilots could return to jobs. Union leaders Bavis and Duffy proposed the pilots call off the strike and salvage whatever jobs were left, but they underestimated the strength of the pilots convictions and their hatred of Frank Lorenzo. The rank-and-file rebelled, kicked Bavis out of his job as head of the executive council and replaced him with the more militant Skip Copeland. Had the pilots agreed to make the best of the situation at Eastern at that point, things *might* have turned out differently—but early polarization techniques were too deeply embedded for that to happen. Symbolically, they had taken a blood oath to destroy Frank Lorenzo *at any cost*!

COMMUNICATION STRATEGIES OF PILOTS AND MANAGEMENT

Pilot Responses

An analysis of the agitation activities of the pilots of Eastern Airlines prior to the 1989 walkout revealed that overall agitation activity was higher in 1986 and 1988 than in 1987. Figure 1 illustrates the pattern of agitation behavior over time. The trend line shows two increased levels of agitative behavior in 1986, a time marked by pilots' interest in confounding the acquisition by Texas Air. The low level of agitative behavior in 1987 reflects the period of "relative peace" identified earlier in this study. An abrupt increase in 1988 continued until the first quarter of 1989 when agitative activity dropped to half that of the preceding quarter.[4]

Five of the eight strategies defined as agitative in the Bowers and Ochs model were identified in the analysis. Escalation/confrontation emerged as the largest strategy overall, with 33 percent of the total activities falling into that category. This strategy was most extensive during the period immediately preceding the pilot walkout. Other representative categories included polarization (29%), promulgation (15%), petition (12.5%) and solidification (10%).[5]

A closer examination of the strategies within each of the three stages prior to the strike shows that the resistance stage, which included weak solidification tactics, resulted in surrender and a return to petitioning tactics. Conversely, the rebellion stage, which was preceded by strong solidification and polarization efforts, resulted in a walkout. The purpose of polarization is to move uncommitteed individuals "into the agitation ranks."[6]

Figure 1

Frequency of Agitation Activity by Quarter Years January 1986 Through March 1989

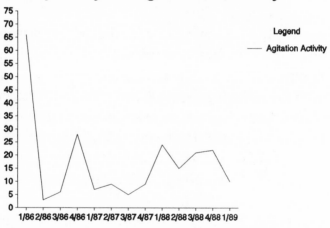

By using the employees' fear and hatred of Frank Lorenzo to their advantage, pilot leaders effectively polarized their constituency and crystallized any neutral attitudes to their way of thinking.

Management Responses

Bowers and Ochs defined *control* as the response of the decision-making establishment to agitation.[7] The definition suggests a strong positive correlation between agitation and control activities. That suggestion was supported in previous research when a comparison of the overall strategies used by each side resulted in high, positive correlation. The trendline, as reflected in Figure 2, reveals one departure from this pattern. During the first quarter of 1988, the pilots' agitative activity increased sharply.[8] Management's response, however, seemed to lag.

By way of explanation, it is possible that management, lulled by the somewhat diminished level of agitation activity, simply was slow to respond to what turned out to be a rebellious progression of behavior. Another possibility is that corporate communications, intent on making the employees the first to know of organizational events, could not respond quickly enough to agitative activities conducted by the pilots via the faster mass media networks.

All three categories of control strategies—adjustment, avoidance, and suppression—appeared in this study. As predicted, avoidance behavior dominated the other strategies. Suppression was evident but difficult to detect because Eastern's management was not likely to jeopardize company image by publicizing any suppressive activity. To do so may have focused public sympathy on the plight of the pilots and other employees.[9]

Figure 2

Frequency of Agitation and Control Actions by Quarter Years from January 1986 Through March 1989

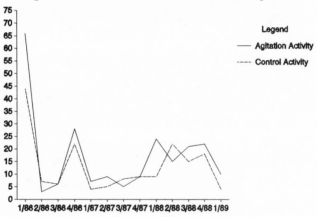

Agitation and Control Activity

Legend
— Agitation Activity
---- Control Activity

CONCLUSIONS

This study set out to determine whether the demise of Eastern Airlines was preceded by detectable patterns of conflict between the pilots and management. Detectable patterns emerged in this study in the form of two striking characterizations of the Eastern conflict. First, as agitative activities increased, Eastern's management maintained a steadfast avoidance posture. Adjustment tactics were seldom employed, and suppression, although evident, was used considerably less often than avoidance. In effect, Eastern adopted an unwaivering stance in response to pilots' demands for change. Second, a closer examination of the pilots' agitative strategies during each of the phases showed that the rebellion was preceded by intense polarization efforts. While this research makes no attempt to determine causality, the relative strength of the agitation strategy of polarization prior to the Rebellion may pique the interest of researchers interested in turning points of collective actions.

It is interesting to note, in the observance of social change, that the less agitative strategies of petition, promulgation, solidification, and polarization seem to rely more heavily on verbal tactics than do the later strategies. The highly agitative stages of nonviolence resistance, escalation/confrontation, and guerilla often involve public nonverbal acts of defiance and seem to communicate a commitment to the cause, no matter what the cost. This notion of "cost to the agitator" should be explored further within the organizational context.

For example, our society generally accepts certain acts of social protest. Certain behaviors (speaking out, carrying protest signs, or even chaining one's self to the gates of a nuclear plant) can usually be conducted without fear of condemnation. Other behaviors are not so widely tolerated (i.e., animal rights activists throwing blood onto people wearing fur coats, or slashing furs with razors). *Within organizations, however, the point at which a behavior starts to "cost" an agitator* is less clear. Generally speaking, agitative behavior within an organization becomes risky at an earlier stage. As a result, it is possible that certain behaviors indicate a stronger commitment to an organizational cause than those behaviors would indicate in a social setting. Had the management of Eastern Airlines been cognizant of this, they would never have underestimated the pilots' willingness to walk.

The communication professional interested in proactively handling organizational crises would do well to pay attention to the phase identified in this book as "Relative Peace." The solidification/polarization efforts during that period contributed to the pilots' level of commitment. Those interested in the area of crisis management, which has little research in intraorganizational communication, will find this case study useful.

The pilot walkout at Eastern Airlines was an act of organizational rebellion, pure and simple. Their sole intent in supporting the machinists' strike was to overthrow Frank Lorenzo, and they were committed to this end whatever the cost. In the end, the cost was dear.

> And he gathered them together into a place called . . . Armageddon.
> Revelation 16:16

NOTES

1. John Waite Bowers and Donovan Ochs, *The Rhetoric of Agitation and Control* (Reading, Mass.: Addison-Wesley, 1971), 141.

2. Aaron Bernstein, *Grounded: Frank Lorenzo and the Destruction of Eastern Airlines* (New York: Simon and Schuster, 1990), 234.

3. Martha Saunders, "Eastern's Employee Communication Crisis," *Public Relations Review* 14 (Summer 1988): 36.

4. Martha Saunders, "Eastern's Pilot Rebellion: Patterns of Conflict Rhetoric Preceding the 1989 Pilot Walkout at Eastern Airlines," (Ph.D diss., The Florida State University, 1990), 88.

5. Saunders, "Eastern's Pilot Rebellion," 88.

6. Bowers and Ochs, 20.

7. Bowers and Ochs, 4.

8. Saunders, "Eastern's Pilot Rebellion," 119.

9. Saunders, "Eastern's Pilot Rebellion," 119.

SELECTED BIBLOGRAPHY

Associated Press. "Flight Crew Has No New Clues on Jetliner That Cracked Open." *The Miami Herald*, February 13, 1988, A1.

Bavis, Captain Jack. "Master Chairman's Report." *Eastern Pilot's Checklist*, April 1988, 15.

Bavis, Jack, Dan Vician, and Buzz Wright. "Support Your Eastern Pilot's Hostage Fund." *Eastern Pilot's Checklist*, April 1988, 15.

Bernstein, Aaron. *Grounded: Frank Lorenzo and the Destruction of Eastern Airlines*. New York: Simon and Schuster, 1990.

Birger, Larry. "Lorenzo Will Be Tough but His Determination Is What Eastern Needs." *The Miami Herald*, June 9, 1986, BM5.

Bowers, John Waite, and Donovan J. Ochs. *The Rhetoric of Agitation and Control*. Reading, Mass.: Addison-Wesley, 1971.

Breslin, Captain Bob. "The Bottom of the Morality Barrel." *Eastern Pilot's Checklist*, June 19, 1987, 16.

Broderick, Pat. "A Fed-Up Pilot Speaks Out." *Newsweek*, April 23, 1990, 8.

Buckley, William F. "Eastern Still Exudes Special Allure." *Pensacola News Journal*, June 20, 1989, A7.

Cerabino, Frank. "Eastern Jet Cracks Open on Landing in Pensacola." *The Miami Herald*, December 29, 1987, A1.

Ennis, Michael. "Sky King." *Business Month Magazine*, September 1988.

Fairley, Henry. "Air Sickness." *The New Republic*, June 5, 1989, 21.

Field, David. "Nader Affiliates Warn Eastern Return Risky." *The Washington Times*, July 28, 1989, A12.

Fields, Gregg. "Judge: EAL Can't Hire Orion As Backup." *The Miami Herald*, 30 March 1988, B4.

Gambardella, Andy. "Thirty Pieces of Silver." *Eastern Pilot's Checklist*, May 1988, 13.

Goman, Carol Kinsey. *Strategies to Excel in Changing Times*. Berkeley, Calif.: Kinsey Consulting Services, 1986.

Gordon, Judith R. *A Diagnostic Approach to Organizational Behavior*. 2d ed. Boston, Mass.: Allyn and Bacon, 1987.

Gordon, Marcy. "Eastern's Not Out of Woods Yet." *Pensacola News Journal*, December 24, 1989, D1.

Hall, Jeffrey R. "Are Pilots Wimps?" *Eastern Pilot's Checklist*, February/March 1988, 8-9.

Hoffmeyer, Ronald. "Another of Our Wounded Pauses to Say Goodbye." *Eastern Pilot's Checklist*, February/March 1988, 9.

Huckabee, Captain Don. "The Fall of Eastern: Lorenzo's Legacy." *Air Line Pilot*, 60 (March 1991): 10.

Kornhauser, Arthur, Robert Dubin, and Arthur M. Ross, eds. *Industrial Conflict*. New York: McGraw-Hill, 1954.

Leff, Laurel. "Texas Air Chief Not a Hero to All: Tough Tactics Earn Lorenzo Reputation as Union Buster." *The Miami Herald*, February 24, 1986, A8.

Lyons, David. "My Gold Parachute Failed, Pilot Says." *The Miami Herald*, August 8, 1986, C5.

_____. "Eastern's Labor Chief Expected to Leave." The *Miami Herald*, August 14, 1986, D7.

_____. "Eastern's Unions Up the Ante: Offer Concessions and $1.15 Billion." *The Miami Herald*, November 20. 1986, D7.

_____. "EAL Meeting Erupts in Chaos: Merger OK'D." *The Miami Herald*, November 26, 1986, A1.

_____. "Lorenzo Sends Regrets to Labor Leaders." The *Miami Herald*, December 24, 1986, B4.

_____. "Eastern Antagonists Play Out Final Drama." *The Miami Herald*, January 19, 1987, B7.

_____. "Eastern Pilots Rap Sick Rules: Management Says It's Curbing Abuse." *The Miami Herald*, January 28, 1987, B5.

_____. "More Eastern Pilots Bailing Out." *The Miami Herald*, March 10, 1987, B5.

_____. "Eastern Workers Feel the Iron Fist." *The Miami Herald*, March 29, 1987, C1.

_____. "Eastern to Layoff 3,000." *The Miami Herald*, November 11, 1987, A1.

_____. "EAL Pilots Threaten Walkout, Atlanta Deal Riles Union." *The Miami Herald*, February 12, 1988, A1.

_____. "EAL Acknowledges Deal with Orion." The *Miami Herald*, February 13, 1988, D5.

_____. "Lorenzo: Texas Air Chief Offers Last Hope to Eastern." *The Miami Herald*, October 30, 1988, F1.

_____. "For Managers, Cuts Are Key to Survival." *The Miami Herald*, December 4, 1988, F1.

_____. "Pilots May Back Walkout." *The Miami Herald*, February 10, 1989, F16.

_____, and Martin Merzer. "Eastern to Stay Put, Buyer Says: Sale to Texas Air Shocks Employees." *The Miami Herald*, February 25, 1986, A1.

Merzer, Martin, and David Lyons. "Did Eastern Prolong Labor Crisis? Tough Negotiating Tactics May Have Been Used to Impress Buyer." *The Miami*

Herald, March 1, 1986, A1.

Moorman, Robert. "Eastern Pilots Sign New Pact." *The Miami Herald*, December 24, 1986, B4.

Oden, Kenneth J. "A Memo to Management from One of the Junkyard Dogs." *Eastern Pilot's Checklist*, November-December 1988, 2.

Reed, Ted. "Chief Eastern Protagonists Take a Back Seat." *The Miami Herald*, June 18, 1989, F1.

Rickenbacker, Captain Eddie. "I Believe in Prayer." Reprinted from *Guideposts Magazine*, 1945, in *Eastern Pilot's Checklist*, January 1989, 26-27.

Satterfield, David. "Eastern Pilots to Deluge D.C. with Postcards." *The Miami Herald*, June 11, 1987, C6.

Saunders, Martha. "Eastern's Employee Communication Crisis." *Public Relations Review* 14 (Summer 1988): 33-44.

Saunders, Martha. "Eastern's Pilot Rebellion: Patterns of Conflict Preceding the 1989 Walkout." Ph.D. diss., The Florida State University, 1990.

Scott, Joe. "Our Basic Obligation Is to Run Profitable Airline." *The Falcon*, March 5, 1986, 1.

Serling, Robert J. *From the Captain to the Colonel: An Informal History of Eastern Airlines.* New York: Dial Press, 1980.

Summers, Lawrence H. "A Traveler's Lament." *Eastern Pilot's Checklist*, April 1988, 3.

Stockton, William. "Tearing Apart Eastern Airlines." *New York Times Magazine*, November 6, 1988, 36-39.

Thomas, Paulette. "Bumpy Ride: Pilots Feel the Stress of Turmoil in the Airline Industry." *The Wall Street Journal*, April 24, 1987, 3(1).

Tomb, Geoffrey and Arnold Markowitz. "Pieces of Engine Fall From Plane, Start Fire." *The Miami Herald*, February 16, 1988, A1.

U.S. Department of Labor, Bureau of Labor Statistics. *Monthly Labor Review.* Washington, D.C.: U.S. Department of Labor, Bureau of Labor Statistics, 1989.

INDEX

About the Author

MARTHA DUNAGIN SAUNDERS is Assistant Professor in the Communication Arts Department of the University of West Florida in Pensacola. She holds a Ph.D. in communication theory and research from Florida State University.